FUTURE LEADER

FUTURE LEADER

Rebooting Leadership to Win the Millennial and Tech Future

JONATHAN WILSON

SANDCASTLE PUBLISHING

For information about this title, or to order other books and/or electronic media, contact the author.
Jonathan Wilson at Jonathan@SandcastleCompany.com
www.JonathanWilson.co

Library of Congress Control Number: 2018907048

Print ISBN: 978-0-9998136-0-7
Electronic ISBN: 978-0-9998136-1-4

Printed in the United States of America

Cover design and interior layout by Longfeather Book Design
Interior illustrations by Laura Braddick
Editing by Jim Thomsen
Editing/Proofreading by Julie Hersum
Indexing by Debbie Olson

Don't tell me the moon is shining;
show me the glint of light on broken glass.

— Anton Chekhov

CONTENTS

Why You Should Read This Book
in 1,323 Carefully Chosen Words xi

Part I: The Case for the Future Leader

1. The Clarion Call for the Future Leader 3
2. Leadership on the Rocks 11
3. The Force of Generational Churn 29
4. The Force of Rapid Technological Advancement 45
5. Win the Future 65

Part II: The Future Leadership Framework

6. **CREATIVITY:** The future leader's ability to continuously find and respond to the right problems 71
7. Mission: Find the Right Problems to Solve 73
8. Synthesis: Create Stories from Data 89
9. Strategy: Set the Organization's Sail 103

10. **INTERACTIVITY:** The future leader's ability to enroll members of the future organization 119
11. Relationships: Develop the Currency of the Future Organization 123

12. Empathy: Use Emotional Intelligence to Move Others . 137
13. Trust: Be Radically Transparent 149

14. **PRODUCTIVITY:** The future leader's ability to generate results in the future organization 161
15. Expectations: Provide Abundant Clarity 163
16. Teams: Harness the Power of Future Teams 175
17. Training: Grow Your Greatest Asset 189
18. Organization: Establish a Robust System of Organization 203

19. **SUMMARY** 215

Part III: Future Leader Quick Start Guide

20. Future Leader Quick Start Guide 223
21. Take the Future Leader Assessment 225
22. Get Insanely Organized 239
23. Renew the Mission 247
24. Future Leader Success Plan 253

About the Author 257
Taking the Future Leadership Framework Beyond the Page . . 259
Special Thanks 261
Notes 263
Index 287

FUTURE LEADER

Why You Should Read This Book

IN 1,323 CAREFULLY CHOSEN WORDS

ALEX HONNOLD ACCOMPLISHED something nobody else had. Alex is a Millennial, and in 2017 he free-solo climbed the 3,000-foot granite rock formation, El Capitan, in Yosemite National Park. In only three hours and fifty-six minutes he made it to the top using only his hands and his feet and a bag of chalk. This type of climbing requires perfection attained through years of experience and practice. If you're not perfect, you'll die.

When I first read about Alex's climb, I felt my palms sweat. My anxiety swelled when I saw a picture of Alex hanging high up on the side of the wall with only his ability to rely on. I am in awe of Alex, but not for obvious reasons. Yes, he successfully conquered a tough challenge. Yes, his feat is one for the record books. But, for me, what is more awe-inspiring is the realization of who Alex had to become to make such an attempt in the first place.

We are deeply moved by others who dedicate time, energy, and attention to develop ability. Nobody begins their rock climbing career with El Capitan. Nobody begins playing guitar on a stage in front of a crowd. Nobody builds a hot rod after buying their first set of wrenches. Alex put in the time, energy, and attention necessary to master the skills and, hence, the ability to summit El Cap. That is awe-inspiring.

THE FUTURE LEADER

Like rock climbers, future leaders also need to develop a distinct set of abilities. Future leaders, for the sake of this book, are not young people in entry-level roles learning skills to someday become leaders themselves. This book isn't necessarily focused on turning the next generation of task technicians into great leaders, although that may be a by-product.

The focus of this book is to provide existing leaders at all rungs on the proverbial ladder with the knowledge and the tools to help their organizations transition to a future that will be heavily influenced by generational changes, as well as technological advancement.

The phrase "future leader" in this book becomes a noun. It becomes a way to distinguish between those who are employing the same old tired leadership hacks that don't work from those who have rebooted the fundamentals of leadership to meet the demands of the current business landscape.

Future leaders are those of us who have widened our gaze enough to see that the workplace and the environment surrounding that workplace are rapidly shifting. Future leaders can see that the framework for effective leadership cannot remain stagnant while everything else is changing. Future leaders are willing to make uncomfortable changes because they want to succeed and they want their organizations to succeed.

And, to be sure, a successful organization—success defined here as consistent and measurable progress toward its mission—always hinges on its leaders' abilities.

Time is tight these days, and there are many skills the future leader could learn. Which ones should they learn? The answer, of course, is dependent on the times, and times are changing.

THE TWO FORCES

Anyone can calculate force in the physical world by multiplying the variables of mass and velocity. Increase mass or increase speed or increase both and the potential force of a thing also increases. A train traveling at full speed down the tracks can generate more force than a car pacing the train on a parallel street would. They might be going the same speed, but the train has more mass.

Force, is the term I have applied to two distinct and external agents that we are familiar with but that are only now starting to significantly agitate the workplace. These agents are considered external because they are outside your organization's ability to control. These agents are generational churn and rapid technological advancement.

Force #1: Generational Churn

The force of generational churn is the movement of the generations through the workplace. We have reached a point at which the older, second-largest generation ever, the Baby Boomers, are starting to retire in waves while the younger, largest generation ever, the Millennials, continue migrating into and up through our organizations.

For almost three decades, things were relatively stable as the 70 million-plus Boomers—those born from 1946 to 1964—occupied the office buildings. The sheer number of Boomers generated enough influence in the workplace to create distinct cultural expectations. Because of their population size, and because this cohort moved through organizations as a group at the same time, they inadvertently created a steady and stabilizing effect on the workplace. Over time, this effect has made us feel a bit too comfortable. We think that the workplace customs, traditions, and expectations, among other variables, are some business absolute. In fact, we have been hypnotized. Instead of an absolute, the workplace is actually just a composition of Boomer tastes and preferences that have solidified over time.

The swinging jewel that has hypnotized us for so long is quickly coming to a dead stop. Boomers are reaching retirement age in staggering numbers just as the last of the Millennials are reaching the age of twenty-one in staggering numbers. There is a wholesale changing of the guard happening in the wider workforce as both the Boomers and the Millennials enter life's next chapters. Generational churn as a force is becoming more pronounced because of the size of the affected population (mass) multiplied by the speed at which the turnover is happening (velocity). Generational churn used to be more like the car and now it is more like the train.

Force #2: Rapid Technological Advancement

Generational churn, though, isn't the only train speeding along on the tracks. Organizations are also dealing with the force of rapid technological advancement. This force is about accelerating technology that is changing what the work can be, and how that work gets done. Factories are moving from human labor to automated labor and seeing massive productivity gains. Law firms are using artificial intelligence programs to perform research once conducted by humans. Several companies are working on autonomous vehicles that will move people and goods around without a human driver.

Just as we have reached a point on the overall human timeline where there is a massive changing of the generational guard, so too have we reached a point where the technology of today is finally catching up to its science-fiction potential. Technological advancement, like generational churn, is also becoming more like the train and less like the car.

The issue for future leaders when it comes to advancing technology will not be the technology itself. Technology becomes the bright and shiny object that distracts us. The underlying issue for future leaders is how to blend technology and people in such a way that the organization makes faster progress toward its larger mission.

As technology continues to make its inevitable improvements, organizations will look to their future leaders to navigate the implications. What will it mean for the mission of the organization? What will it mean for labor? What should it mean? These aren't questions for tomorrow, they're for today. Leaders who aren't seriously asking these questions, and many others, are already behind the curve.

* * *

THE NEXT TEN YEARS will look very different from the past ten years. Generational churn will continue to take its toll. Technological advancements that are influencing productivity and profitability will continue to alter how our organizations go about their business. Future leaders will need a playbook to navigate these challenges.

Just as it was for Alex climbing El Capitan, the harder the challenge, the more ability you will need. This book is designed to help you gain that ability by focusing your time, energy, and attention on the skills our organizations will need in the years ahead.

The future waits for no one. It's time to get started.

Part I

THE CASE FOR THE FUTURE LEADER

1

The Clarion Call for the Future Leader

WE NEED YOU NOW MORE THAN EVER BEFORE

"THEY AREN'T GOING TO LISTEN, and even if they do listen, they aren't going to do anything about it." The voice of Resistance was being firm with me.

Resistance is that little voice in your head that does everything it can to derail creative effort. Resistance, as used here, is a concept credited to author Steven Pressfield. Resistance says stuff like, "Who are you to do this?" and, "Why should anyone listen to you?" and, "This stuff is complete garbage. Maybe you should think about it some more before sharing it with anyone." It's that small but persistent voice that has the ability to sit right down in your soul. The voice of Resistance has always been strong with me, and it was talking to me again while I was driving to the event a few years ago.

In an effort to give Resistance an identity, I have turned it into a late-fifties man with a stubbly face and an overweight body. The tan and cream striped shirt he is wearing paired with the brown shorts and the socked feet in loafers is a clue that he stopped keeping up sometime in the late 1970s. When he has something to say, I always imagine he has an iced tea in his hand and he is just telling it like it is. For some reason, Mr. Resistance lives in perpetual summer in my mind. There is something powerful about the contrast of nice weather and a "realistic" perspective.

As I pulled into the parking lot that day, I slapped him in the face and returned my thoughts to the presentation I was about to make. My goal was to try to persuade over a hundred of my mostly Boomer colleagues and superiors that we needed to do more to prepare for the younger generations than we had been doing. As an organization, we tended to hire Boomers for senior leadership roles. The senior leaders would then look for other Boomers to fill staff positions. Generation X, the generation just younger than the Boomers (and the generation I am in), was tolerated. Millennials, the generation just younger than Generation X, probably felt as if they were from another planet. We were an old-school organization with a massive blind spot about generational change.

If you have ever ridden a roller coaster, there is a certain feeling you can relate to. You see the drop-off coming and can do nothing about it. If generational issues were like this roller coaster approaching the drop-off, then the senior leadership at the organization I worked for decided that their best response was to hold on tight to the handlebar and squeeze their eyes shut. Soon the scary part would be over and those Millennials would just go away.

What I tried to persuade my colleagues to understand was that the roller coaster drop-off they were trying so hard to ride out actually continues down forever. The underlying message for my mostly Boomer audience was that their time of dominance in the workplace was over, and we would be wise to embrace the change. This is something to lean into, as Sheryl Sandberg might say, not something to ignore. To do this, I argued, we first had to make the mental shift to a new mindset, and then a physical shift that resulted in action.

GENERATIONAL ISSUES ARE DIFFERENT NOW

Sitting in my car at the community center after the event had concluded, I thought more about the problem. Generational issues in the workplace are nothing new. People in different generations have different ideas and perspectives about the world. We see things differently. We do things differently. We have different expectations. And all of these differences, as we will see in Chapter Three, are based in science.

The generational friction we see in the workplace now, however, is on steroids. We are in the middle of a massive transition in the workplace that is creating structural turnover. This turnover is happening as the second-largest generation ever to occupy the workplace, the Boomers, gives way to the largest generation ever, the Millennials. Generation X, the much smaller generation in-between, is basically along for the ride.

The confusion, chaos, backbiting, adaptation, and overall friction found in a number of organizations as these massive generations slide past each other is powering what I call the "force of generational churn." Like the force of an earthquake that happens as two land masses rapidly slide past each other, so too is the force of generational churn shaking up our organizations. Congratulations! You have a front-row seat to biggest changing of the guard ever to happen, and it is taking place right now in every organization.

The official dethroning of the Boomers as the largest generation represented in the workplace has happened only within the last few years. The consequences will play out for years to come. Boomers typically hold higher-level positions than Millennials due to their age. Boomers have had more time in the workforce to move up the corporate ladder.

This dynamic will continue to fuel an unequal allocation of power over the next several years. Boomers will be outnumbered in the office by Millennials—like, by a lot—but a number of Boomers will still sit in the corner offices. Millennials will occupy almost every other desk in the office but may not necessarily have the formal organizational power that comes with a job title. At least not yet. Can you see how tricky this might be?

The presentation I gave that day worked, but I learned later that I missed a big part of the overall problem. What I missed in that presentation to my colleagues while I was all wrapped up in generational issues was that there is another significant force working relentlessly to permanently reshape our organizations. This force is just as powerful, if not more powerful, than the force of generational churn, and it is also just as underappreciated. The second substantial force agitating all organizations is what I call the "force of rapid technological advancement."

TECHNOLOGY IS ALSO DIFFERENT NOW

It's not technology in and of itself that is the issue. We all love our iPhones and our laptops. We appreciate driving a car or riding mass transit to work instead of whipping a horse.

The issue for future leaders is how to blend technology and people in such a way that the organization makes faster progress toward its larger mission. Technology is the only mechanism out there that can fundamentally reshape and redefine what business is and how it gets done.

Think about it for a moment. The largest provider of rides in the world is a company that owns no cars. The largest provider of places for people to stay owns no buildings. These are two obvious examples of how advancing technology is changing not only what our work can be, but how we live our lives.

We are on the leading edge of creating autonomous vehicles. Imagine being able to travel to work in an Uber or a Lyft with no driver. Seems really cool! But the excitement that comes with pioneering technology should give way to a fundamental question: How do opportunities for organizations to fulfill their missions change as technology improves?

Think about where we were just ten years ago. Twitter and Facebook were in their infancy. Instagram and a number of other social platforms weren't even in existence yet. Organizations employed no social media managers or strategists. Social media was still just for fun.

Steve Jobs announced the first iPhone about ten years ago. Remember the phone you had before your iPhone? Texting was a nightmare on the old flip phones!

Ride-sharing companies like Uber and Lyft were nowhere to be found. Airbnb was not in existence yet. Tesla was only a few years old in 2007, but no Teslas were on the road. Amazon didn't sell everything. The best artificial intelligence (AI) at the time was a far cry from the AI we have now.

In addition, the workplace was still in the capable hands of the Baby Boomer generation. No Boomer had reached age sixty-five ten years ago, and the oldest Millennials were only in their mid-twenties. The workplace was still in its period of generational stability. Things felt solid and safe and predictable ten years ago. Doesn't that feel like yesterday? Now, fast-forward ten years from today.

In the next ten years, we will be taking for granted new technologies that don't exist yet. AI will continue to step, maybe leap, forward in complementing or supplanting human labor. New organizations will offer technology not invented as of this writing, and other organizations that have been around seemingly forever will fade away as they fail to adequately respond to the two forces. The youngest Boomers will be about sixty-four years old and the vast majority of that generation will have moved into retirement. Meanwhile, the Millennials will be *the* generation in the workplace with its membership reaching the powerhouse years of their late twenties to late forties.

WE NEED FUTURE LEADERS

Right now, more than ever before, we need the future leader. Rock-solid, authentic, and motivating leadership tuned to the times will be key to organizations making successful generational and technological transitions.

There is no more room for scientific management, management by spreadsheets, or any other leadership model that is not specifically designed to deal with the forces of generational churn and rapid technological advancement. As we will see in the next chapter, leadership in its current form is on the rocks. By a number of measurements, what has passed for leadership has harmed our organizations as much, if not more, than it has helped. And, these problematic models of leadership are now being further agitated by the forces of generational churn and rapid technological advancement.

Senior leadership in organizations from all industries should be on red alert when it comes to their leadership at this moment on the human timeline. The next ten years will be pivotal. In no other time has the quality of leadership had as direct a role in keeping the organization alive than now.

All of this boils down to a central question: What will it take to effectively lead the future organization? The answer is a rebooted leadership model.

WE NEED A NEW LEADERSHIP FRAMEWORK

Leadership is about moving people to action on a mission. This feels like it should be easy, but doing it well has never been. It won't become easier. A proper response to leadership that is already underperforming and that is being further influenced by the forces of generational churn and rapid technological advancement is rebooting the basics. We don't need a digital solution to this analog problem, we need a better analog solution. The Future Leadership Framework is that solution.

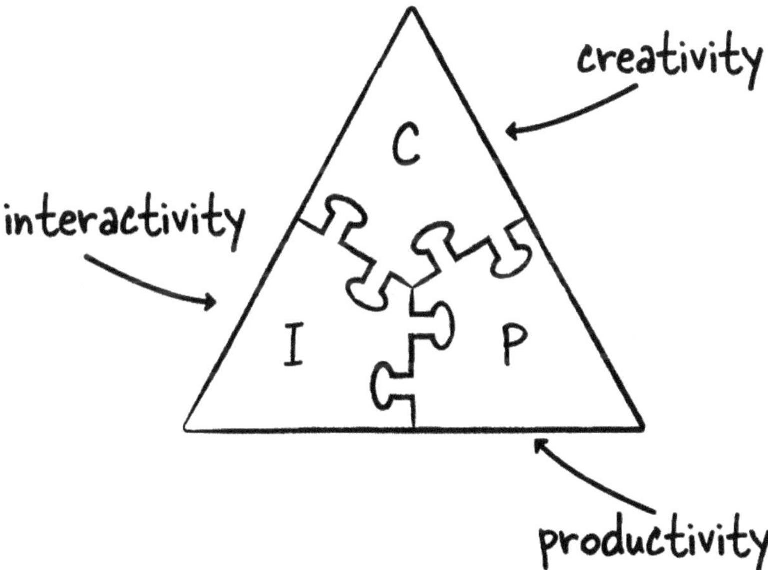

As you will see in Part II of this book, the Future Leadership Framework is a collection of skills that any leader can master.

These skills will help offset the forces of generational churn and rapid technological advancement so that your organization has a better shot at success.

The ten skills coming in Part II of this book are grouped into three abilities. The idea is that once you have mastered the skills, you will gain the corresponding abilities. These abilities will be required of all future leaders responsible for transitioning their organizations successfully to the future.

Before we can move into the solution, though, we must first understand the problem. In medicine, the disease informs the prescription. In leadership, it's the same way. Let's start with looking at the state of leadership today. I think you will be surprised at what the research has uncovered.

KEY IDEA

What has passed for leadership up until now has created a number of underperforming organizations. The difference now is that these leadership models are being further agitated by the forces of generational churn and rapid technological advancement. The result may prove disastrous. The solution is not a new leadership model. The solution is a rebooted leadership model designed to be the antidote to underperforming leadership and the two forces.

2

Leadership on the Rocks

MEASURING THE OUTCOMES OF LEADERSHIP

"ANYONE FALLING SHORT after two months would be fired." This is a quote in a 2013 story in the *Los Angeles Times* about the company culture at Wells Fargo.[1] Wells Fargo is a commercial bank that was founded by Henry Wells and William Fargo in 1852 in San Francisco. It originally catered to the gold-mining community, but has since grown considerably in its scope and size. Wells Fargo is the fifth-biggest public company in the world with $1.9 trillion in assets and serving more than 70 million customers in 8,400 locations.[2]

The article caught the attention of the Los Angeles City Attorney, Michael Feuer. He quoted one passage from that article about Wells Fargo in his testimony for the Senate Committee on Banking, Housing, and Urban Affairs. "To meet quotas, employees have opened unneeded accounts for customers, ordered credit cards without customers' permission and forged client signatures on paperwork. Some employees begged family members to open ghost accounts."[3] "Appalled" at what he read in that article, Feuer started an investigation.

As with a number of other organizations, the problems that caught the eye of the LA City Attorney are leadership problems.

In general, bad leadership should be thought of as a cancer that can affect organizations of any size, even the largest and most prosperous. Two-person organizations are just as easily affected as two-hundred-thousand-person organizations.

The LA City Attorney's office concluded its investigation in 2015 and found that:

> *...the Bank [Wells Fargo] victimized consumers by opening customer accounts, and issuing credit cards and other products, without authorization. Further, we found that the Bank failed to notify customers that these accounts had been opened without their consent and failed to refund fees incurred by those customers for these unwanted products and services. We found instances in which the Bank made it difficult, if not impossible, for customers to receive accurate and clear information as to how this happened. Many were told that the unauthorized accounts would be closed, only to find later that they were not.*[4]

The line staff in the branches of Wells Fargo did not open unauthorized new accounts for customers just because. Behavior like this always comes from somewhere. Feuer noted that "... Wells Fargo's business model imposed unrealistic sales quotas that, among other things, incentivized employees to engage in highly aggressive sales practices, creating the conditions for unlawful activity..."[5] In whatever way, the company's expectations, as communicated, had the effect of encouraging behavior that was both contrary to the law and the bank's long-term interest. As Scott Reckard says in his *Los Angeles Times* article that caught Feuer's attention: "The relentless pressure to sell has battered employee morale and led to ethical breaches, customer complaints and labor lawsuits."[6]

Leadership failures at Wells Fargo will be really expensive. As of this writing they are already on the hook for $185 million in fines in addition to restitution to the victims.[7] *CNN Money* reports that restitution will amount to $142 million.[8] While this is an awesome example of the high cost of underperforming leadership, the cancer of bad leadership is evident in a number of organizations.

Leadership failures at the now-defunct Enron cost investors billions of dollars, took down one of the "Big Five" accounting firms, Arthur Andersen, and resulted in criminal convictions for a number of Enron's senior leadership. Leadership failures at VW led to 11 million cars being outfitted with "defeat devices" that helped them beat emission testing for nitrogen oxides.[9] VW has reportedly set aside $6.8 billion to deal with the problem.[10]

Keeping a business going is tough enough without having to deal with something completely avoidable like bad leadership. The Small Business Administration notes that small businesses—composed of 500 or fewer employees—make up 99.9 percent of all businesses in the United States.[11] They also note that from 2005 to 2015, almost 80 percent of these organizations managed to survive at least one year.[12] That is encouraging, but as the years go on the chances for survival take a nose dive. Only about half of organizations make it to five years, and only about a third make it to ten years.[13] These stats aren't as bad as some in politics have made them out to be, but they still illuminate a harsh reality. Keeping a business going, in general, is difficult. We don't need to make it any harder.

There's a cure for cancerous leadership that costs organizations valuable resources. But before we can appreciate that solution, we have to better understand the problem. Fortunately, bad leadership leaves behind clues. The case studies noted above provided clues that are extreme and obvious, but other clues can be so subtle that many of us have unintentionally grown accustomed to their presence.

What clues should we be looking for?

LEADERSHIP ALWAYS LEAVES CLUES TO ITS EFFICACY

The best clues as to the effectiveness of leadership are found in the outcomes of that leadership. Before we look at the outcomes, though, we must be crystal clear on something fundamental and important: If you are a leader, every problem in your organization is your problem. Deciding to become a leader means you have signed up for this level of responsibility. Your people are your problem. How well the product is selling is your problem. Customer service is your problem. The computers going down is your problem. People with sullen faces walking around the office? Your problem.

This maxim holds even if there is clear and compelling evidence that it is not your problem. The reason everything is your problem is because the fate of the organization in whole depends on you. The buck stops with you. Sorry to lay it on so heavy, but it is really important that we are clear on where the ultimate responsibility lands.

Now, back to measurement. To properly assess leadership quality, we should look at the clues, or outcomes of that leadership on the organization. We want to understand how people are responding to their leadership.

Outcome #1: We Are Disengaged and Bored

One big way to measure the outcome of leadership is by looking at employee engagement. Engaged employees are emotionally and mentally invested in the work they do and the organization they do it for. Disengaged employees tend not to be emotionally or mentally invested in the work. The main motivation of the engaged is progress on their team's mission and the organization's mission. The main motivation of the disengaged is to collect pay for time.

Gallup has been polling Americans since the 1930s and is now in the business of collecting, analyzing, and providing actionable data to organizations. As of this writing, Gallup is showing that only 13 percent of the worldwide workforce is engaged at work.[14] In the United States, only 32 percent of the workforce is engaged.[15]

This is an alarming statistic. The scales are tipped wildly in the direction of the disengaged. The next time you're in the office, look around. Despite how they might be reacting in the moment, two out of every three people you see are disengaged from their work. Engagement, either positive or negative, is a big deal because it affects morale, productivity, and ultimately the organization's bottom line. Low employee engagement is a clue.

A close relative of employee engagement is boredom. Are your team members bored at work? Recently, the online training company, Udemy, completed a workplace-boredom study. Its findings: 43 percent of American office workers are bored at work, and Millennials are twice as likely to be bored at work as Baby Boomers.[16]

This is a problem because bored employees are twice as likely to leave the workplace. The main reason that survey respondents cited? Not enough learning opportunities. The next reason: the work was unchallenging and didn't use their education.[17]

Boredom is a tough issue in the workplace. Some jobs, by their very nature, will be less emotionally, mentally, or physically engaging than others. Some leaders would tell you that it is fine to be bored at work because somehow that's what they pay you for.

This sentiment just won't fly any longer. To attract skilled talent in tight labor markets means employers will need to think through the jobs they offer. In addition, the skilled talent your organization needs won't tolerate tedium as easily as older generations did. Boredom at work is another clue.

Outcome #2: We Are Unclear about What Is Expected from Us

Engagement and boredom are decent metrics to evaluate the efficacy of organizational leadership, but there are even more fundamental indicators about whether leadership is doing its job. One of my favorites concerns employee expectations.

Do you actually know what is expected of you at work? Think about it. Do you really know, or do you just have an idea? There is a big difference. One analysis of workplace expectations found that only 50 percent of people strongly agree that they know what is expected of them at work.[18] Half! The rest of us may have some idea what is expected of us, or no idea.

To be clear, expectations are not contained in job descriptions. Rather, they are fluid. They correspond to the initiatives the team is working on, and the initiatives the organization is working on. Both are subject to change and, therefore, the expectations are also subject to change. What was expected of you last quarter or last year may not be expected of you now.

If we don't know what is expected of us, then we can't adjust our behavior to meet or exceed those expectations. We will continue to do what we have always done, and the gulf between what is expected and what we are actually doing may continue to widen.

This is not only a rank-and-file problem. The research noted above also reported that 50 percent of managers are unclear about what is expected of them.[19] Wow! The fact that only half of us know what is expected of us is another clue.

Outcome #3: We Aren't Getting Enough Feedback

A symbiotic relationship exists between expectations and feedback. If expectations for your team members were never set in the first place, then it can be difficult to provide feedback about their work. Missing expectations usually leads to ineffective feedback, and not getting enough feedback is a problem.

OfficeVibe offers tools to empower managers to create better workplaces. OfficeVibe reports that managers aren't giving enough feedback, and the feedback they do give is either too negative or too vague.[20] Their report also finds that 65 percent of employees want more feedback while 58 percent of managers think they provide enough feedback.[21] In the workplace, there is a disconnect between how much feedback we want and how much feedback we get. The net effect is that we are left without enough information to make the necessary changes to our performance. Productivity suffers as a result.

I have always believed that receiving feedback is much easier than giving it. A number of other leaders may feel the same way. Despite this proclivity, the OfficeVibe report notes that 82 percent of employees appreciate feedback, whether it is positive or negative.[22] The research is telling us that we, as leaders, shouldn't be uncomfortable about providing feedback. It is also telling us that we need to provide more of it.

Clutch is a company that matches companies looking to complete projects with companies willing to do those projects. In 2016, Clutch surveyed 1,000 full-time workers about their job fulfillment. This survey found that 72 percent of Millennials whose managers provided accurate and consistent feedback rated their jobs as fulfilling.[23] What about the Millennials who didn't receive accurate or consistent feedback? Only 38 percent found their jobs fulfilling.[24] In their analysis, Clutch goes on to note that workplace experiences can be improved for Millennial employees simply by creating a better system for providing feedback.[25]

Gallup has also looked at Millennials and feedback and notes in their report, *How Millennials Want to Work and Live*, that less than one in five Millennials say they receive routine feedback, and even less report that the feedback they do receive is meaningful.[26]

The evidence shows that workers from all generations, especially the Millennials, want more feedback than they're currently getting. The evidence is also showing that the feedback we are getting is not as helpful as it could be. Not enough feedback and feedback that is unclear are clues.

Outcome #4: We Don't Know the Vision, Mission, Strategy, or Goals

If I asked you to tell me what the vision and mission of your organization is, could you do it? You may know what the organization does day in and day out, but that is not the same as its mission. Achievers, a company that makes employee recognition and rewards programs, conducted a study of several hundred people in the United States, Canada, and the United Kingdom in 2014. In their 2015 report based on that study, Achievers noted that 70 percent of respondents didn't know either their company's vision or mission.[27]

If you have read a typical mission statement, you can probably understand why it isn't memorable. Many of these statements are forgotten as soon as they are read, often times a direct result of too many boring business buzzwords mushed together in unclear or meaningless sentences.

The same problem exists for strategy. Like vision and mission, an organization's strategy can also be unmemorable. When employees were queried a similar percentage of them who couldn't recall the vision or mission also couldn't pick their organization's strategy out of a lineup. One research initiative focused on employees at twenty major corporations in five industries in Australia. The researchers noted that all of the companies had established competitors, large market shares, and had articulated public strategies.[28] The researchers had employees of these organizations look at six strategy statements and asked each of them to pick out the one that best fit their firm. Anyone off the street has about a 17 percent chance of picking the right strategy statement just from luck alone. It turns out that these employees fared only slightly better than you or I could have—only about 29 percent were able to make the right selection.[29]

Separate research about organizational goals done by the authors of the book, *The 4 Disciplines of Execution*, echoed the theme of employees being unfamiliar with the basics of their organizations. The authors' research found that only 15 percent of those surveyed could name one of their organizations top three most important goals.[30]

The point is evident. Whether we are talking about the vision and mission of the organization, the organization's strategies, or the organization's goals, a vast majority of employees whose job is to execute on these items simply don't know what they are. How can we expect them to be successful?

A general misunderstanding of the "why" (vision and mission) and the "how" (strategies and goals) of the organization is another clue.

Outcome #5: We Don't Trust Our Organizations

There is another powerful indicator of leadership's efficacy, one that's just as basic as whether you know the organization's vision, mission, strategy, or goals, but carries more weight. This indicator is trust.

Do you trust the organization you work for? Trust is delicate. It takes time to create and can evaporate in an instant. In any organization, trust is both established and wrecked by its leadership. Edelman, a public-relations firm, released the sixteenth edition of the *Edelman Trust Barometer* in 2016. One dimension Edelman focused on in its report was the state of trust between employers and employees. The results are less than encouraging.

According to Edelman, only 64 percent of executives, 51 percent of managers, and 48 percent of the rank-and-file trust the organizations they work for.[31] Trust trends downward from the corner office to everybody else. Overall, Edelman reports that only about two-thirds of us trust the company we work for.[32]

Edelman isn't the only company looking at the issue of trust in the workplace. EY is a large business professional services firm that recently released its third annual survey of generational issues in the workplace. The focus of this survey was on trust.

The survey of almost 10,000 adults working full-time at companies in eight countries, and 3,200 minor workers (age 16 to 18), came to a different conclusion than Edelman. According to this survey, only 46 percent of global respondents had a "great deal of trust" in their current employers. The survey also noted that about 17 percent of respondents had very little or no trust in their employer.[33]

Trust mingles closely with employee engagement. The two affect productivity and, in turn, organizational profitability. When leaders create an environment that hampers trust, they also create an organization that is at a competitive disadvantage. The level of distrust in a number of organizations is another clue.

Outcome #6: The Culture at Work Is Unhealthy

Let's look at organizational culture. Culture is composed of values, beliefs, attitudes, and behaviors that influences how people work together. Culture is essentially how we do things 'round here. Cultures originate and are reinforced by an organization's leadership.

One of the ways the culture of a workplace can be measured is by the health of the people who work there. Kronos is a company that provides tools "to manage and engage your entire workforce from pre-hire to retire."[34] This organization partnered with Future Workplace and recently completed a survey of hundreds of HR professionals from organizations with at least one hundred employees. What they found was that almost half of all HR leaders reported that burnout is responsible for up to half (20 to 50 percent, specifically) of their annual turnover.[35] The study found that the top three contributors to burnout were unfair compensation (41 percent), unreasonable workload (32 percent), and too much overtime (32 percent).[36]

A *Harvard Business Review* article noted that the psychological and physical problems of burned-out employees cost an estimated $125 billion to $190 billion in healthcare spending annually.[37] The article goes on to note that the real cost can be much higher because burn-out lowers organizational productivity and creates higher than necessary turnover, including the loss of an organization's most capable talent.

As we will see in a later chapter, taking care of your team has direct benefits to your organization. Attracting skilled talent in the tight labor market of 2018 is much harder than attracting that same talent in the economic desert of 2008. Additionally, unnecessary turnover of high-performing team members is expensive. The expense is not just in the direct costs of replacing somebody and the extra hours that everybody else has to put in to make up for the absence. The expense also comes from the opportunity costs. Organizations that intentionally or unintentionally promote a culture of burnout aren't winning the short-term and they aren't winning the long-term either. It's a classic lose-lose scenario. A culture of burnout is another clue.

Outcome #7: And We Can't Even Take a Break

An organization's culture also impacts how its employees use their vacation time, and right now we aren't taking as much vacation as we used to. The average American took only 16.8 days off from work in 2016, which might seem high until you put it in context. From 1976 to 2000 Americans averaged over 20 days off.[38]

The question is: Why aren't we taking as much vacation as we used to? The answer points back to leadership. More than 25 percent of us fear that taking a vacation could make us appear less dedicated.[39] More than 20 percent of us worry we might miss out on a raise or a promotion if we dared spend too much time away from our desks.[40]

Now, before you are too quick to blame the problem on the person who is not taking the vacation, consider where these notions are coming from. A full two-thirds of us say that our company culture is "ambivalent, discouraging, or sends mixed messages about time off…"[41] If the dominant culture at an organization frowns on vacations, the employees will pick up on it and adjust their vacation expectations accordingly.

Author and happiness researcher, Shawn Achor, has studied the effects of vacation and found that vacations make you happier and less stressed (true!), and that by taking a vacation you can return to work with more energy.[42] Company culture that dissuades the use of vacation, even though there are bottom-line benefits that come from employees who take time off, is another clue.

THE CLUES POINT TO UNDERPERFORMING LEADERSHIP

The clues we have uncovered so far show that:

1. A vast majority of us are **disengaged** from our work;
2. We are **bored** with our work, and the turnover associated with boredom is a problem;
3. We are unclear about what is **expected** from us at work;
4. There is not enough **feedback**, and the feedback we do receive is not helpful;
5. A majority of us don't understand the basics of the organization, such as its **vision**, **mission**, **strategy,** and **goals**;
6. Too many of us don't **trust** our organizations, and by extension, our organization's leadership; and
7. The **culture** of the workplace is creating conditions leading to overwork, burnout, and turnover.

By looking at the outcomes of today's leadership, we have a clearer picture of its efficacy. Those outcomes show that the models we are using right now to lead our teams are actually working against us, and they are working against our organization's best interests. Leadership in a number of organizations cultivates workplace conditions that encourage underperformance resulting in unnecessarily high turnover, missed opportunities, and wasted money and time.

Underperforming Leadership Costs the Organization Time and Money

None of this is about the treatment of people for the sake of humanity, although treating people well should go without saying. Rather, each of the outcomes of leadership described above have bottom-line implications.

Underperforming leadership is expensive.

Let's look at employee engagement as an example. Leadership that moves workers from disengaged to engaged results in dramatic productivity and profitability improvements. One analysis found that organizations with higher employee engagement beat organizations with lower employee engagement by over 20 percent in both productivity and profitability. And, the organizations with higher employee engagement experienced less turnover and less absenteeism.[43]

Disengaged employees in the aggregate are costly. Actively disengaged employees cost American organizations up to $550 billion annually in lost productivity.[44] To put that number into a larger context: this one issue alone is equivalent to almost 2.4

percent of the total United States GDP! To put that number into a smaller context, consider that employee disengagement is costing American organizations about $4,366.22 per employee, per year.[45]

Engagement versus disengagement is a huge problem for modern employers and the quality of the organization's leadership plays a significant role. Leadership also plays a significant role influencing the organization's overall productivity. A 2002 survey of 1,300 private-sector companies found that, on average, only 59 percent of work time is productive. Researchers attribute this to three major causes: insufficient planning and control, inadequate management, and poor working morale.[46] This equates to a five day workweek in which only three days are productive.

What about the costs of turnover? There's a saying that people don't leave their positions, they leave their bosses. I have firsthand experience that tells me this is true, but research also backs up this claim. It turns out that half of us have left our job at some point to get away from our manager and to improve our quality of life.[47] The job is fine, the commute is fine, the health insurance is fine, the coworkers are fine, but the boss was too much to handle. Skilled talent that quits because of bad leadership is expensive.

The Society for Human Resource Management's recent Human Capital Benchmarking Report concludes that the cost to fill an open position averaged $4,129 and took forty-two days to complete.[48] A Center for American Progress article noted that the actual turnover costs varied somewhat depending on the salary and skills of the worker.[49] For instance, those who made $30,000 or less cost less to replace than executives. The article noted that replacing a worker costs about 20 percent of that worker's annual salary.[50] So, for a worker who makes $50,000 per year, the cost of turnover is about $10,000. Absent from these figures, however, is the opportunity cost that comes from missing an employee, and the morale hit that the team may experience if each member's workload increases. The actual total cost of turnover as a result could be even higher.

All of this research probably just confirms something you know in your gut to be true.

Leadership is a key component to the success or the failure of any organization.

We know that leadership right now is on the rocks, but is this all we should know about the topic? I believe there is something else everyone who has been entrusted to lead should understand.

LEADERSHIP AND THE TWO FORCES

Over the next ten years, organizations of all sizes and in all industries will be grappling with two key, rapidly intensifying external agents. These agents will add significant pressure to organizations and their leadership models. The result is that organizations already dealing with significant leadership challenges will be further agitated. Agitating leadership that is already underperforming could result in slow-motion disasters for a number of organizations.

The external agents are the force of generational churn and the force of rapid technological advancement. These two forces are working to reshape and redefine what the organization looks like and how it functions. To better understand the scope and scale of these forces, the next two chapters will examine them in detail.

KEY IDEA

The only way we can measure whether leadership is working or not is to look at the outcomes of that leadership. The outcomes, as shown in the research, are demonstrating that leadership in a number of organizations is underperforming. Leadership that is already underperforming will be further agitated by two external forces rapidly increasing in intensity: generational churn and rapid technological advancement.

3

The Force of Generational Churn

THE MOVEMENT OF THE GENERATIONS

HUMANS INSTINCTUALLY categorize and label things. We have named all of the oceans in the world even though they are all connected. We have named the continents and even artificially divided them into distinct countries. Countries have become further divided and labeled. The United States, for instance, is divided into fifty states, and then into smaller counties, and then into smaller cities, and then into the neighborhoods that make up the cities. We have names for the stars in the sky and have arranged these stars into clusters called constellations. We have named all the animal species we have found thus far and even have a system for categorizing these animals.

THE POWER OF PATTERNS AND PATTERNICITY

Why do we do this? It turns out that our motivation to categorize and label things is built into our human operating system. The fundamental function of the brain is to encode and integrate the internal and external information coming from our senses, and then create a behavioral response.[1] In the context of the brain,

Hey, pattern-seeing superhero...

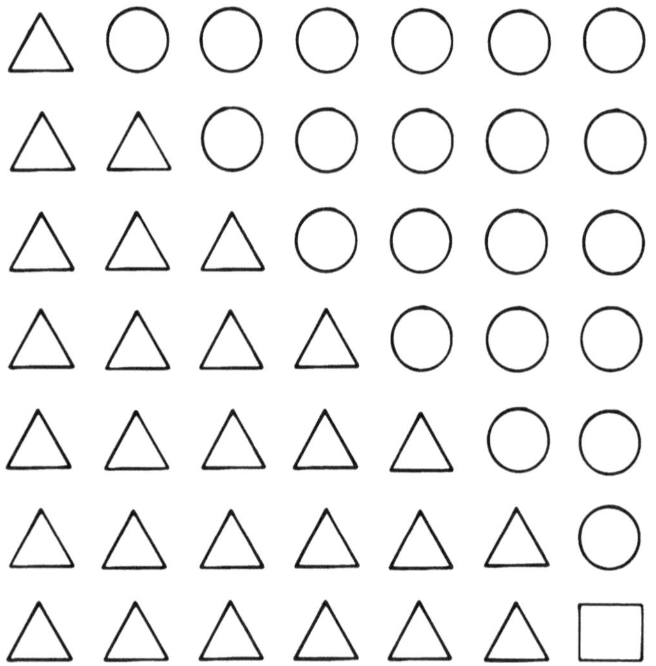

Where's the error?

encoding is the process of converting raw information into useful information. The encoding process starts by looking for any patterns in the information.[2]

The superpower of humans is taking raw information and turning it into useful information by finding patterns. In fact, we are so good at finding patterns that there is a term—patternicity—that explains the phenomenon of seeing patterns where none truly exist.[3] Patternicity happens when someone sees the face of Jesus in a grilled-cheese sandwich, for instance.

Just as we categorize and label the stars and animals, so too do we tend to categorize and label people. We judge people by the clothes they wear, the college they attended, the car they drive, the words that come out of their mouth, the energy they exude, and a variety of other factors. Where is this human tendency most evident? High school.

One of my favorite scenes in the movie *Ferris Bueller's Day Off* is the scene where Principal Rooney is talking to his administrative assistant, Grace. He is explaining to Grace why Ferris Bueller is a bad role model. Her response rebuts what he is saying and confirms how popular Ferris is. She says, "the sportos, the motorheads, geeks, sluts, bloods, wasteoids, dweebies, dickheads, they all adore him. They think he is a righteous dude."

High school, though, is only where our tendency to categorize and label is most flamboyant. After high school is over, a great many of us quietly (or not so quietly) continue this behavior simply because we are biologically programmed to do so.

Humans use their superpower of pattern recognition in an effort to better understand. Pattern recognition has powered the fields of sociology, psychology, and astrology, among others, and pattern recognition has also powered research into the generations. At some point we identified the existence of cultural and behavioral patterns among groups of people, and the concept of the generations was born.

THE GENERATIONS? REMIND ME

A generation is a collection of people who have all been born during a certain period of time, usually about twenty years. The only prerequisite for membership in any generation is your age. While generations researchers haven't unified on the exact years the different generations' begin and end, most researchers have pegged these dates in a relatively narrow range. As of 2018, five generations are currently present in the workplace. Some generations have way more representation in the workplace than others because of their relative size or because of their constituents' age.

Generations

	Birth Years	Population
Traditionalist	1925 to 1942	~ 29 million
Baby Boomer	1943 to 1964	~ 75 million
Generation X	1965 to 1979	~ 61 million
Millennial	1980 to 2000	~ 83 million
Generation Z	2000 to ?	~ 75 million

In the chart above, I included years of birth for each generation. They're a bit misleading. Think of these groups as occupying areas on a spectrum instead of points on a distinct timeline. In a visible light spectrum, there is no delineated edge where yellow ends and red begins. They blend, and eventually the color turns from one to the other. It's the same with the generations. Researchers set artificial boundaries for each generation according to birth year, but the boundaries, in reality, are fuzzy. You may find yourself "misplaced" by your birth year into a generation and a corresponding set of characteristics that doesn't describe you. That happens.

With respect to the caveat mentioned above, you are likely to have some or all of characteristics of your generation. There is a certain milieu that resides in each generation that helps to distinguish its members. It's like a club where all the members wear the same pin or the same hat. Millennials don't wear the same hat as the Boomers, or Generation X, or the Traditionalists. They are from different clubs.

The research has repeatedly shown that each generation has its own beliefs, cultural norms, and perspective of the world. The notion of the generations is not about the differences between young people and old people. Rather, the notion is that we are fundamentally different because we grew up at different times on the overall human timeline.

Thus, our superpower has helped us to recognize the patterns among the people born during a relatively short span, and then to categorize those people into groups we call the generations. However, what our superpower hasn't done is help us answer a basic question: *Why* do the people who make up each generation have similar outlooks, beliefs, and ways of doing things?

"IMPRESSIONABLE YOUTH" IS MORE THAN A PHRASE

Mrs. Pancho was crying. I remember being in my third-grade classroom. I was only eight years old on January 28, 1986, and when I think back on that day, I can't seem to make all the pieces fit. I remember a lot of people crying, and I also remember how the smoke looked.

I saw the loop on television later that day after school. The Challenger shuttle was just a minute past takeoff when it exploded over the Atlantic Ocean. All seven people on board, including teacher Christa McAuliffe, were killed. *The New York Times* called it one of the worst accidents in the American space program.[4]

I wish I could say that I learned the invaluable lesson about the fragility of life that day, but I didn't. My takeaway was that the world was a big place and I was just one very small piece of that big place. That event sparked a certain awareness that I hadn't had before. The Challenger disaster helped inform my natural view of the world, and it is often decisive events like this that happen in our formative years that shape our beliefs, perspectives, and attitudes as adults.

The people who grew up during the Great Depression have a much different view about money than people who have not gone through such a period of hardship. The people who served in Vietnam as teenagers and early twenty-somethings have a different view about armed conflict than people who have never served.

Karl Mannheim, who many refer to as fathering the concept of the generations, wrote a dense essay called the "Problem of Generations." As a sociologist, Mannheim stated that:

> *...in estimating the biographical significance of a particular experience, it is important to know whether it is undergone by an individual as a decisive childhood experience, or later in life, superimposed upon other basic and early impressions. Early impressions tend to coalesce into a natural view of the world. All later experiences then tend to receive their meaning from this original set...*[5]

How our attitudes and views are shaped by events depends on when we experience them in our lives. Significant events in early life set the stage for contextualizing other events later in life. This is why the essential differences between generations are not between the ideas and behaviors of younger people as opposed to older people. Instead, there are fundamental differences between a Traditionalist and a Gen Xer because each has experienced different events in their youth that "coalesced into a natural view of the world."

Imagine American babies born in the early 1990s. These babies, by virtue of their dates of birth, are assigned to the Millennial generation. When these Millennials were eight years old, another significant life-shaping event took place: the terrorist attacks of September 11, 2001. I watched the space shuttle explode when I was eight years old, these eight-year-olds saw airplanes flying into buildings.

Think of the impression this made on these children in their formative years, versus the impression it made on those of us who were adults. As a twenty-something watching the continuing coverage of 9/11, I saw a man, still clutching his briefcase, jump from near the top of one of the burning buildings. Imagine an eight-year-old watching the same thing.

Those kids who experienced 9/11 as eight-year-olds are now in their mid-twenties. How has that event and the subsequent fallout shaped their natural view of the world? The kids who experienced 9/11 grew up with a prolonged war in the Middle East, the economic downturn of the early 2000s, new security procedures for getting on airplanes, and the death of Osama bin Laden. The influence of terrorism that has overshadowed their youth has shaped and informed their worldview in some way.

When an event happens to us is equally, if not more, important than *what* the specific event is when it comes to shaping our particular views of the world.

GENERATIONAL INFLUENCE ON THE WORKPLACE

The strength of any generation is a direct function of its population. In other words, the larger the generation in terms of pure bodies, the more influence that generation has. The Baby Boomers, at one time the largest generation ever, have been capitalizing on their influence for the last three decades. We may think that the ethos of the modern office is some business absolute, but in reality, the office culture, customs, dress codes, beliefs, and work processes, among other things, are all just products of Boomer preferences. The reason you work from eight a.m. until five p.m. in an office that takes you forty-five minutes to commute to (even though you could do that same work from your dining room table) is because this arrangement is what many Boomers prefer, and they have had the influence to enforce its adoption.

Because Boomers have had the population numbers to generate significant influence, the workplace culture has bent to their will, and then remained in its new configuration for decades as the Boomers worked their way through the system. The difference now, however, is that generational representation in the workplace is fundamentally changing because Boomers are retiring.

In fact, Millennials, as of the first quarter in 2015, are officially the largest generation represented in the workplace.[6] The proverbial baton of influence is being passed (not necessarily willingly) from the Boomers to Millennials, and we have front-row seats to watch this epic transition unfold.

Understanding generational representation in the workplace is key for future leaders. As Millennial representation increases, its influence on the workplace will also increase. The preferences of Boomers with respect to the customs and traditions within the office cannot remain intact as their influence ebbs. The question isn't about whether things will change, but what the change will look like. Change is inevitable.

What makes this transition of influence even more eye-opening is the democratizing effects of the internet. Karl Mannheim could not see from his vantage point how the internet would change the world. Mannheim commented on the power of "similar location" in his paper on the generations. He said that members of a generation were similarly located if they were all exposed to the same phase of the collective process.[7] In Mannheim's time, people of a similar age and social strata who grew up in the same geographical location were similarly located, and that would help explain the underpinnings of a generation. Mannheim goes on: "It is not difficult to see why mere chronological contemporaneity cannot of itself produce a common generation location. No one, for example, would assert that there was community of location between the young people of China and Germany about 1800."[8] Yes, Karl, I would not assert that about youth in the 1800s, but I would absolutely assert that there is more "community of location" in 2018 because of the internet. Now it is possible to get close enough to the experiences that help shape our natural views of the world wherever they occur. And, it is also possible to get close enough to great cat videos.

Right now, half of the world's population uses the internet. That number has risen almost 1,000 percent since the turn of the century and will continue to rise as new technologies increase access.[9] What this trend means is that the generations coming up will be much larger in scale, and hence more influential, than past generations. A Gen Z in the United States and a Gen Z in the United Kingdom or China may be more alike than we realize.

GENERATIONAL CHURN IS A FORCE

In the physical world, force is the product when mass is multiplied by velocity. For a thing in motion, the higher the mass or the velocity (or both), the more force that thing will generate. Generational churn is the phrase I use to describe the effects of Baby Boomer retirements coupled with the rise of the Millennial generation. Generational churn becomes a significant force on the workplace because of the amount of people involved in the churn (mass) multiplied by the speed at which the churn is happening (velocity).

Earlier we noted that the Boomer generation—people aged 54 to 75—was the largest generation ever to walk the planet, and for decades, was the largest generation represented in the workplace. Over the next decade, 10,000 Boomers will turn sixty-five each day.[10] While not everyone who reaches retirement age automatically drops out of the working world, a number of them will. The official retirement age for Americans is sixty-six, but the average retiree is only sixty-three.[11]

The Bureau of Labor Statistics says that members of the Boomer generation tend to stick with jobs longer than members of other generations. They report that the average tenure for a Boomer is more than ten years.[12] A longer duration of employment means Boomers have been able to dig a deeper well of institutional knowledge. Institutional knowledge is the almost instinctual ability to get things done in an organization that can only come from years of experience. The longer you work somewhere, the more you know about that organization and its ecosystem. You know the internal, informal power structures better, and you know which vendors are reliable and which aren't. You know what good work looks like, and you deeply understand the organization's culture.

When someone who has been with an organization for ten

or fifteen years leaves, a period of chaos ensues. Even if the retiree is replaced with someone who has the exact same qualifications and experience, there will still be a gap that takes time to close. Employees lose mentors. Vendors lose trusted contacts. Customers lose long-term relationships. Each retirement opens up a new chasm that the organization must fill. If you take what happens with a single retirement in a single organization and multiply it by thousands of people in thousands of organizations, the problem grows considerably in scale. Now, consider that this retirement wave continues day after day. It seemingly never breaks, it only continues to swell. The effects of this massive wave of retirements is taking a significant toll.

Retiring Boomers are only half of the equation, though. Millennials have been flooding *into* organizations for some time now. We saw above that Millennials have stolen the wrestling-style World Champion belt away from the Boomers as the largest generation ever to walk the planet. And, unlike the Boomers, Millennials are truly the world's first global generation powered by the internet.

Millennials are a wave of another kind. Though this generation is bigger than the Boomer generation, it is not much bigger. Just as about 10,000 Boomers reach retirement age each day, so too are about 10,000 Millennials turning twenty-one each day.[13] This is a trend that will continue for the next three years or so. So, as one big generation moves off the scene, another even larger generation is coming into its own. And, over the next few years, this rapid change will be even more pronounced. One source estimates that by 2020—just two years from now—half of the workforce will be Millennials.[14] That would mean half of the people in your office would be between twenty and forty years old. The generational representation trend continues upward for Millennials. By 2025, Millennials are expected to represent about 75 percent of the workforce.[15]

Different Generations, Different Preferences

While the Baby Boomer and Millennial generations have size in common, that is about all they share. Before we get into the differences, I want to make something clear. All groups are made up of individuals, and individuals are entitled to their own preferences. Generations researchers can make general assertions about the appetites of different generational groups as a whole, but there will always be variation among any generation's membership. With that clarification in mind, researchers have found very different preferences among the generations.

JOB TENURE. One point of differentiation is in job tenure. The Millennials are still in the first chapters of their working life and they don't tend hold a job as long as the older generations do. The Bureau of Labor Statistics finds that the average tenure for someone aged 25 to 34 is only 2.8 years.[16] While the issue of short tenures feels like a long-term problem, we just don't know yet if it is a by-product of relative youth. It could be that the average job tenure will increase as this generation matures. What we do know is that shorter tenures usually equate to shallower institutional knowledge wells.

COMMUNICATION. If you have worked for Boomers, then you have likely attended their meetings. I remember the death-march meetings in which a dozen of us sat around a big table waiting for our turn to update the group on what we were working on. Because of the composition of our department, nobody really understood or cared about what anybody else was working on, except for the Boomer in charge of the meeting. Face-to-face communication tends to be big with Boomers, while Millennials prefer to communicate electronically. One survey of more than

4,000 Millennials noted that more than four in ten preferred to communicate electronically at work.[17] To a Boomer, it may feel weird not to have the weekly in-person status meeting but to a Millennial there may be nothing weird about its absence. It's simply a different preference.

PROGRESSION. Boomers tend to place more value on the concept of "paying dues" than the Millennials. It's not uncommon for some promotions to take several years or even decades to materialize. The Millennials don't necessarily have this kind of patience. Millennials tend to favor advancing more quickly. One survey found that over half of all Millennials see career progression as the primary attractant of an employer.[18] Millennials' preference for quick advancement rubs some Boomers—many of whom may have been biding their time in less-than-ideal jobs—the wrong way. Some think Millennials have an entitlement problem. Instead, couldn't it be that Boomers just have different assumptions and preferences than the Millennials?

OTHER NOTABLES:

1. Where members of the Boomer generation may prefer "standard" working hours and showing up on time, Millennials may prefer nonstandard working hours and self-directed schedules.

2. Where Boomers may prefer to keep the office clean and professional, Millennials may prefer to add more personality to their working spaces. (For instance, try searching Google for "Zappos office," and then look at the images).

3. Where Boomers may value traditional professional attire, Millennials may want more flexibility in the way they dress for work without being judged for it.

We could add more to this list, but what's really important here is to look past the preferences and focus on what the difference in preferences represents. In a word, the force of generational churn is about change, and change is a strong provocateur.

For the future leader, understanding that massive change is afoot and that there are differences in preferences among the generations is half the battle. Successful future leaders don't resist change simply because it's change. Instead, they evaluate all change from a different vantage point.

For instance, if the emerging preference in your organization favors flexible working hours, a successful future leader will recognize that this warrants a thoughtfully considered response instead of a knee-jerk decision based on their own preferences or the preferences of those in senior leadership positions. Successful future leaders will step outside of their own preferences to see the larger workplace dynamic. Only then can they make decisions that work to take advantage of the force of generational churn.

Boomers (and probably the rest of us, too) need to be cognizant that their preferences aren't absolute truth, only relative truth. Gen-Xers need to be cognizant of the significant flux at both ends of the organization and roll with the chaos. Millennials may like to move fast and break things, but they need to understand that the rest of the organization may not feel comfortable moving that quickly. It's possible that the same organization may feel a little stuffy to a Millennial, a little too loose for a Boomer, and a little more irritating to the Gen-Xers.

More than being cognizant, though, is that future leaders must act on what they are seeing. With the rise of the connected culture, an organization refusing to change as the times dictate will not only alienate a large percentage of the younger workforce, but suffer in reputation.

Leaders don't need to fight change, instead they need to embrace it. Leaders also don't need to throw leadership spaghetti at the wall and see what sticks. That is what comes from reading too many internet articles that countdown the "7 Ways to Keep Millennials Happy at Work." A more effective approach means adopting a better model of leadership. Skip the simple tactics and reboot the fundamentals in light of conditions on the ground at this moment in your organization. By understanding the force of generational churn on the workplace and the preferences of different generations, the future leader will be better equipped to make more effective leadership decisions in the years ahead.

KEY IDEA

The force of generational churn describes the organizational friction that is created as the Boomers' influence recedes due to retirements and the Millennials influence continues to increase. As generational representation changes, workplace rules and traditions will invariably change as well. Future leaders need to cognizant of the changing workplace preferences, and they must be ready to lead through the transition.

4

The Force of Rapid Technological Advancement

RESHAPING WHAT WORK IS AND HOW IT GETS DONE

In 1968, Bob Noyce and Gordon Moore formed NM Electronics after they left Fairchild Semiconductor. This was the year before Neil Armstrong left his footprints on the moon and on history after flying in a space machine that contained Fairchild components. Less than a year later, NM became Intelco and, eventually, Intel. At eighty-eight, Gordon Moore still holds the chairman emeritus position. He is also the namesake behind Moore's Law.

Intel is most famous for making computer processors. These processors include models like the Pentium, the Xeon, the Celeron, and a number of others. A computer processor collects, interprets, and executes various demands that come from the computer's hardware and software. Think of processors as the brains of our devices. Processors are found in computers, mobile phones, TVs, tablets, and many more devices.

Among other components, every processor will have a number of transistors. Transistors are tiny, electrically powered switches that regulate electrical current. In 1971, Intel developed the 4004, which was the first general-purpose programmable processor on the market.[1] That first processor Intel created had 2,300 transistors on a two-inch silicon wafer.[2] The old philosophical saw of "less is more" does not apply to transistors. For computer processors, more is more. More transistors equals a more awesome device. A truckload of increasingly smaller transistors on a small processor is why your Pixel phone is so incredible.

Leading Intel in the early days, Gordon Moore had a front-row seat to the development of better processors that contained ever more transistors. He could see the trend in processor improvement and wrote a small article for the trade journal *Electronics*. From that article emerged the concept of Moore's Law: that the number of transistors in a densely packed circuit will double about every two years.[3] Moore could see that computers were not only going to improve, they were going to become exponentially better.

Compared to where the processor started, we are now light years ahead. While the first Intel processor had 2,300 transistors, the latest Intel processors have billions of transistors. Billions!

The direct result of exponentially increasing transistors on a circuit board is that electronics are able to become exponentially better as well. Today's computers are radically better than computers from just a decade ago. Computers a decade ago were radically better than computers from the 1990s. The advancement in processor technology has set the stage for the kind of technological advancement that is now acting as a significant force on modern organizations.

THE NONLINEAR CURVE OF TECHNOLOGICAL ADVANCEMENT

If you were to plot technological advancement on a graph, the points, when connected, would create a unique curve. The curve would look similar to the illustration on the opposite page.

As you move farther along to the right on the graph, the

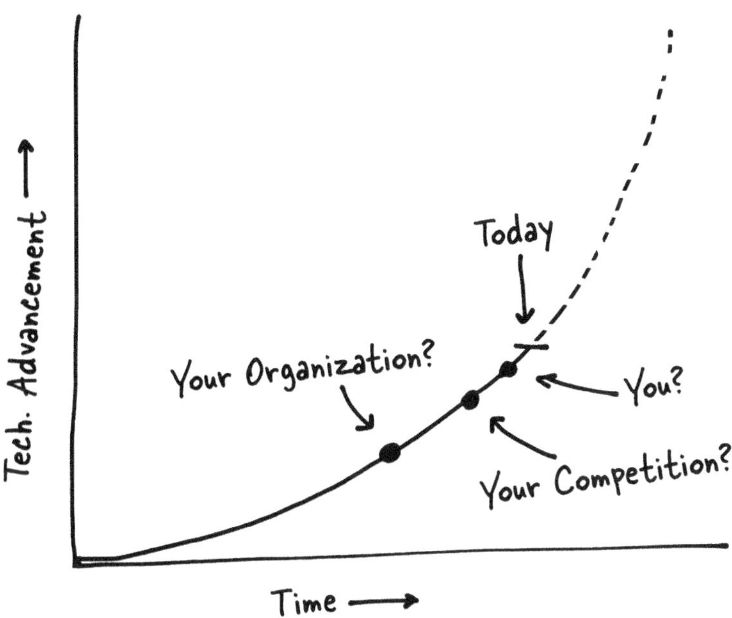

technology gets better, but like Moore's Law for computer processors, this improvement happens at a nonlinear rate. This is why the curve markedly shifts upward the further right you go. Understanding that this technology curve exists, and that it takes this particular shape, is step one for future leaders. Understanding *why* it exists in the first place is step two.

The curve exists for two reasons. The first is that all technological improvements come from some combination of what already exists, and the second is that technological improvements are happening simultaneously.

The Adjacent Possible Powers the Technological Curve

Technology has to be built from something. It simply cannot appear out of a magician's top hat. The "something" that technology gets built on is not only the physical components that make up whatever the technology is, but also the ideas that have been iterated on. It's not possible to skip the iterative process when it comes to technology. We can't run software applications that allow team members to connect with each other from locations around the world without the internet. We can't have the internet without first having the computer. We can't have the computer without first having the components that make up the computer. We can't have those components until we first have the ability to manipulate the raw materials, and so on. All innovation is about collecting, sorting, and stacking what we already have and know to create something new.

The restriction of only being able to move from what is possible to the very next thing that is possible is captured in the concept of the "adjacent possible." It's a phrase credited to Stuart Kauffman, emeritus professor of biochemistry at the University of Pennsylvania.[4] He used the term to describe the potential for enormous biological diversity on earth, but the concept is not reserved for biochemistry.

Author Steven Johnson used this concept to describe where good ideas come from. Johnson says, "think of playing chess: at any point in the game, several ingenious moves may be possible, but countless others won't be. Likewise with inventions: the printing press was only possible—and perhaps only thinkable—once movable type, paper, and ink all existed."[5] The adjacent possible dictates that new ideas, new inventions, and new technologies comes as the result of combining existing ideas, inventions, and technologies.

The adjacent possible affects the speed of technological advancement in two ways. The first way is by making things slow to start. If you look at the left side of the curve you see can see this in effect. The reason things are slow to start is because in the beginning there are relatively few ideas, inventions, and technologies to combine into new ideas.

Technology, though, can advance quickly as the number of ideas to combine into new ideas increases. This is the second way the adjacent possible affects the speed of technological advancement. The adjacent possible keeps innovation slow at the beginning, but then allows innovation to exponentially improve as existing ideas get sorted and stacked into new ideas.

Simultaneous Effort Powers the Technological Curve

The other idea shaping the technological curve is simultaneous effort. This happens when a variety of technologies are iterated upon at the same time. Let's look at this concept in action.

Orville and Wilbur Wright cracked open the door to powered flight at Kitty Hawk, North Carolina, in 1903.[6] The Wright Flyer was a one-person flying machine made of wood and cloth. At Kitty Hawk, the Wright Flyer managed to carry Orville Wright about 120 feet.

Many of us are familiar with the broad stroke of the Wright story. What fewer of us know is that only about ten years later in 1914, the first commercial flight took to the skies in Florida.[7] On New Year's Day in 1914, Abram Pheil, the former mayor of St. Petersburg, Florida, hopped into a biplane operated by Tony Jannus and made the twenty-three-minute trip from St. Petersburg across the bay to Tampa. Pheil paid Jannus for the flight and commercial aviation was born.

The aviation industry rapidly iterated and improved over the next several years, and in 1923, the first nonstop transcontinental flight was made from New York to California in just under twenty-seven hours.[8] Imagine being on a nonstop flight for that long!

In December 1935, just about twenty years after the first commercial flight, the McDonnell Douglas DC-3 was introduced. It could carry up to twenty-eight passengers 1,500 miles at an altitude of 20,000 feet.[9]

The DC-3 was a technical marvel that iterated on a number of advances since the Wright Flyer. Two large radial engines capable of producing 1,200 horsepower each turned the big metal propellers. The DC-3's exterior was constructed from a new aluminum alloy, not wood. Sturdy landing gear helped the giant aircraft take off and return to earth safely. The DC-3 illustrates rapid technological advancement in action, but the story doesn't end there.

About twenty years after the DC-3 hit the market, the Boeing 707 jet aircraft was born. The 707 was another leap for aviation, as it replaced propellers with more powerful jet engines. The 707 was much larger than the DC-3 and could carry up to 181 passengers 3,000 nautical miles.[10] The 707 was way ahead of the DC-3 and light years ahead of the Wright Flyer.

While the story above is narrated in a linear type fashion, the development of aviation technology has been anything but linear. We went from the Wright Flyer carrying one person 120 feet on a windy field in North Carolina to a Boeing 777 that can carry hundreds of people thousands of nautical miles in only 115 years because there were technological advances in aviation happening simultaneously. Whether it was innovation fueled by World War II, or simply by curiosity, different groups of people were working on different parts of a larger problem at the same time.

During this 115 years, some people were specializing in making the wings bigger, better, and more efficient. Other people were specializing in creating the radial engines. Still other people were working on jet engine technology, and so on. Imagine how long it would have taken had the technologists gotten together and decided to work on just one piece of the problem at a time. Linear improvements would preclude us from the comfortable and safe international flights we are able to enjoy today.

Big technological advancements are able to happen fast because they are the product of many small technological advancements happening simultaneously. People are solving small problems all the time and then combining these solutions to solve larger problems. The more problems people solve, the more solutions we have to combine into new ideas. If this concept sounds like a close relative of the adjacent possible, that's because it is. Both of these concepts are required, though, to power rapid technological advancement.

TECHNOLOGICAL ADVANCEMENT IS ABOUT PRODUCTIVITY

With a grasp on the two basic vehicles that allow technology to advance in the first place, we are better poised to understand where technology is going. Now, we need to better understand the integration of technology in the modern workplace.

The role of technology in any workplace is to improve productivity.

Where we might replace our existing mobile device with a new one because of the cool factor, no rational organization invests in new technology because it's cool. Technology can be expensive and often needs to demonstrate a return on investment. The ROI usually comes from productivity improvements that allow the organization to make more money, spend its money more efficiently, or otherwise better execute on its mission. For the past 300 years since the start of the Industrial Revolution, organizations have been adopting technology to generate efficiencies.

Technology Disrupts Manufacturing

A case study in productivity improvements due to technology can be found in the American manufacturing sector. America has had a long romance with the notion of manufacturing. We are nostalgic for the factories that employed millions of people in the middle of the last century. We imagine hardworking men and women on the floors of the factories putting things together with their hands and earning decent pay. Manufacturing is different today.

Right now in America, out of 323 million people, there are about 154 million employed across all sectors. Of the 154 million, about 12.5 million (8 percent) are employed in manufacturing jobs of all kinds.[11] According to the Bureau of Labor Statistics, the number of jobs in manufacturing has been decreasing as a trend line since the late 1970s when manufacturing was at its peak employment of about 20 million people.[12]

Some politicians blame outsourcing: "If we only could keep those jobs from disappearing to lower-wage countries, then everything could return to normal in America." This sentiment still sounds good, but is rapidly becoming nonsense. The real change happening with manufacturing in America isn't outsourcing, it's automation.

What the politicians aren't telling you (and plausibly because they just don't know) is that manufacturing as an industry is actually improving. In fact, manufacturing output in inflation-adjusted dollars has been increasing as a trend ever since the 1920s.[13] Sure, there have been ups and downs when manufacturing output is examined more granularly, but the overall curve for manufacturing output has been relentlessly increasing.

While manufacturing output has been growing, manufacturing jobs have been shrinking. The nuance between manufacturing output and manufacturing jobs is usually where our understanding falters. A *CNN Money* article notes that since the year 2000, America has lost about five million manufacturing jobs.[14] So, the question for the astute observer is: How can manufacturing output go up, while the number of manufacturing jobs goes down? The answer can only be productivity.

A manufacturing employee can produce more now than a manufacturing employee could produce in years past. The credit for this added output goes to better machines, better software, and better processes—in essence, better technology. According to one source, automation and software has doubled the output of each manufacturing employee over the past two decades.[15]

One study on the topic found that about 87 percent of all job losses in manufacturing have been the result of productivity gains. Only about 13 percent have been lost to trade.[16] The manufacturing sector has experienced the productivity horsepower of advancing technology. And, manufacturing output will continue to grow in the years ahead.

The Boston Consulting Group notes that the use of robots for manufacturing tasks will increase to 25 percent in the next seven years from 10 percent today.[17] With respect to manufacturing, companies are producing more than they ever have by using a smaller workforce that is leveraging automation.

Automation Doesn't Take Jobs, It Takes Tasks

The manufacturing case study is a microcosm of the larger issue of technological advancement. What many leaders are missing is that technological advancement isn't an issue we can take up some other time. Technology, and automation in particular, is putting pressure on organizations today. One source estimates that almost one-third of activities people are paid to do can be automated with technology we have available today.[18] What might happen to your organization if your competitors started aggressively putting better technology to use first?

Automation is not about some science-fiction technology that takes jobs away from workers. We aren't talking about a robotic house cleaner like Rosie from *The Jetsons* who puts everything in its place. We are talking about Roomba robots that can assume the singular task of sweeping the floor. Technological advancement is about current and future technology that assumes tasks from workers.

Remember the bored workers we talked about in Chapter 2? Technology is really good at solving for boring by assuming repetitive tasks. A machine won't complain about making the same weld over and over on factory-line car hoods all day long. It just does it. Many jobs aren't quite that narrow, but many jobs are just a collection of tasks that are performed each workday (whether those tasks are boring or not). Reduce the number of tasks that people need to do by automating a portion of the work, and you can reduce the total number of people needed to complete the remaining tasks. As the ratio of machines to people climbs, the balance of organizational inputs invariably shifts.

To be clear, job tasks that are subject to automation are not only physical in nature. We have been talking about factories getting automated, but the concept of automation applies across business sectors. Advances in AI are reshaping a number of white collar jobs as well. The legal industry is one example where AI is promising disruption.

In years past, the law was squarely in the domain of people. The law is about words, the meaning of those words, and critical thinking, not about welding a piece of a car traveling along a factory line. In the legal profession, the human mind is needed for research. People are needed for document review. People are needed to work with the clients. And, while these jobs aren't necessarily going away, a number of individual tasks within the profession may be.

One such company looking to take a few of the tasks off attorneys' plates is Kira Systems. Kira Systems claims to have the "most powerful and accurate contract analysis software."[19] Kira makes a natural language-processing AI that helps lawyers and companies perform quicker and more accurate reviews of contracts and other documents. Where at one time a person, or people, would be required to read and summarize contract documents, now that work can be outsourced to an AI. The *New York Times* notes that the time it takes for contract legal review has been decreased from 20 to 60 percent for clients using Kira software.[20]

The legal field is only one of many being altered by the presence of AI. Another is the travel industry. The promise of AI to make travel simpler and safer is already playing out in a number of airports around the world.

Singapore's new Terminal 4 at Changi International Airport was a billion-dollar project to introduce the concept of FAST—Fast And Seamless Travel.[21] This terminal alone is expected to serve 16 million passengers a year—about the same amount of people that Boston Logan International Airport enplaned in all of 2016.

In Terminal 4, travelers check in using kiosks similar to a number of airports around the world. But in Terminal 4, checking your bags also is automated, as are immigration checks to leave the country. Technology at this airport can scan passports, scan bags, and scan people for security purposes. The machines in Terminal 4 help reduce some of the friction associated with travel. The machines also help reduce the number of employees the airport needs to assist its travelers. And, Changi isn't the only airport to adopt this kind of technology. Other airports around the world are quickly following suit.

Imagine departing from your home airport and not interacting with a single person to facilitate the process. Technology assumes the tasks, and that means potentially fewer jobs.

RAPID TECHNOLOGICAL ADVANCEMENT IS A FORCE

The technological curve coupled with time has created the force of rapid technological advancement. This is a force we are seeing play out in a number of organizations around the world, and this is a force that will only grow in significance.

This force is the product of the proliferation of a variety of technologies (mass) multiplied by the rate of technological advancement due to the expanding adjacent possible and simultaneous effort (velocity). Future leaders who can see the larger story when it comes to technology will be better equipped to handle a rapidly changing future. Technological improvements create a different but equally significant stress on the workplace than the force of generational churn.

The stress on the organization from the force of rapid technological advancement comes from two primary sources. The first source of leadership stress comes from the need to bring organizations out of the technological past and into the present day. The second source of stress will come as future leaders will be required to thoughtfully balance the organization's inputs (humans and technology) based on its desired output (success toward fulfilling its mission).

Future Leaders Need to Transition Their Organizations to the Present and Future

The technological curve we have been talking about has an ultimate limit dictated by time. The curve stops on the graph at today. Of note, though, is that not everybody and not every organization is at the same point along the technological curve. We are not all at "today." Some people have personally incorporated technology that puts them closer to today, but you will also find a number of people who are happy residing in the technological past.

The same is true for organizations. Couple the fact that new technology is expensive with an "if it ain't broke, don't fix it" attitude, and you can understand why some organizations may choose to live in the past. Where an organization exists along the technological curve is neither right nor wrong, it just is. Living in the past becomes a problem, though, when the competition adopts more effective technology that ends up undermining your organization's ability to execute on its mission. In this case, the "do nothing" approach to incorporating new technology equates to falling further behind. What if your main competitor could offer the same service for 30 percent less cost than you could?

There tends to be a big disconnect between how we adopt technology at the personal level versus at the organizational level. While some of us stand in line for the new iPhone, many organizations are standing in a different line for dot-matrix printer parts. OK, it's probably not that bad, but consumer adoption of technology has been speeding up relative to organizational adoption.

Ray Kurzweil is an author and futurist, and he demonstrates the trend of technology adoption in a chart, "The Mass Use of Inventions."[22] He notes that where it took about forty-six years for electricity to reach 25 percent market penetration, succeeding technologies have taken far less time to spread.[23] The personal computer only took sixteen years to reach the same level of adoption. The mobile phone only took thirteen years, and the internet only took seven years. We are adopting new technology quicker now than we have in decades past.

Our organizations are another story. There are plenty of anecdotes out there about people trying to navigate today's work using old technology. While you likely have your own story about workplace technology that seems laughable, there is an underlying problem that a number of us have missed. When organizations refuse to adopt technology that could actually help them better execute on their mission, they end up creating a technological gulf that gets harder to cross with each passing year. These organizations might be stuck using 2005's technology even though we are firmly in 2018. Remember what the tech looked like in 2005?

Author and futurist Ben Hammersley calls this a "presentism" problem. Hammersley asks: What year is your business operating in? He goes on to note that most organizations are somewhere in the past, and how far in the past they are defines the problem they have.[24] For a number of organizations, we aren't yet talking about transitioning them to the future, we are still talking about transitioning them to the present.

The problem of bringing organizations up to the technological "today" is part of the work for future leaders, but the problem doesn't end there. Future leaders also have to instill a new ethos that keeps the organization iterating into the future. If the work done to drag the organization up to the technological present stops, the technological gulf problem will just reappear again in the years hence. The only difference is that the gulf may widen much faster in a much shorter period of time than it did in years past.

Future Leaders Need to Balance Organizational Inputs

As you bring your organization up to today and transition into the future, another key consideration is balancing the technological and human inputs within your organization.

We have reached a time in which future leaders need to carefully assess technological advancements against the organizational mission.

It may be that even though cheaper and better technology could replace a human's touch, the organization decides not to implement the technology because it would detract from the organization's mission. We can illustrate this with an example from Costco.

The Costco near my home has recently installed a kiosk-based ordering system for the food court. On a pedestal away from the cashiering stations are a number of touchscreen displays where people can order pizza slices and hot dogs and churros. You order and pay for your food at the kiosk and then wait to hear your order number called from the pickup station. While the food requires somebody to prepare it, the transaction requires no staff to facilitate. There is no interaction between the face of Costco—its people—and the customer at this particular touchpoint.

Now, I want you to consider this example from the future leader's perspective. Kiosk stations, already popping up in a number of fast-food restaurants, are cheaper, faster, and less prone to mistakes. The kiosk does not call in sick, and does not require breaks or health insurance. On paper, the kiosk is the clear, long-term winner from a bottom-line point of view.

Does this technological alternative, though, best align with the organization's mission? Does replacing an employee who interacts with the customer and has the opportunity to help keep that customer coming back make sense in this particular instance? It might, or it might not. The future leader will have to make that call, and these decisions will become more complicated.

The ordering kiosks are only the opening salvo when it comes to automation in certain businesses. At Costco, let's look at another job that could become automated.

When you enter Costco, there is a person at the entrance. This person acts as a greeter and checks your card as you enter. From what I understand, that person is counting bodies and relaying it to other staff who can then prepare for the approximate demand later on at the checkout lanes. We have technology today that can eliminate the need for that job. Technology can count bodies more reliably and for less cost. Place a sensor above the door and it will perform the counts and relay that information automatically. However, imagine Costco without a greeter.

Next, Costco could implement technology similar to what Amazon has put into its new grocery store in the South Lake Union neighborhood of Seattle. This isn't about creating more of possibly the worst invention of all time—the self-checkout lanes—but about eliminating the cashiering phase of the customer experience altogether. At the Amazon grocery store, you can walk in, grab a bag, fill it with products, and then just walk out. Amazon tracks the interactions you had with their products and emails you a receipt when you leave.[25] Thread these concepts together and you can see a potential future for Costco.

Using kiosks for ordering food removes one of Costco's customer touchpoints. This is probably not a big deal in and of itself. Removing the greeter would take away another customer touchpoint. Maybe this still wouldn't be a big deal. Getting rid of cashiering would be another lost customer touchpoint. Now, is it a big deal? Maybe.

Removing the cashiering experience altogether might be too much of a trade-off against what Costco has identified in its Code of Ethics. Costco's second bullet point in its Code of Ethics says the company will "take care of our members."[26] To elaborate on this bullet, Costco says, "if we don't keep our members happy, little else we do will make a difference."[27] I know this might sound like typical corporate BS, but it is actually true for organizations that depend on returning customers to stay alive.

If most customer touchpoints are automated, though, how does that keep me happy as a Costco member? I don't connect with robots; I connect with people. Maybe Costco starts to feel more like a shed in the backyard where people go in to grab something and then leave. No connection or interaction required. For future leaders balancing the technological and human inputs of implementing these changes, how sticky would you guess I would be as a customer? Would I be more open to competitors since I have less of a human connection? Maybe. Maybe not. Maybe there are a number of us who would love to do their Costco trips without having to interact with anyone. It's a difficult call the future leaders of Costco will have to make.

Future leaders will have the new job of balancing the human and technological inputs to create the best outputs. This hasn't been a significant part of a leader's job up until now. It will be possible in the years ahead to take technology too far, thereby changing how we view and interact with organizations. Incorrectly balancing the inputs has the potential to create more problems than technology can solve.

Future Leaders and the Force of Rapid Technological Advancement

As a future leader, you will need to bring your organization into the technological present, keep your organization in the technological present, and thoughtfully implement a balance of technology and people with the bigger mission of the organization in mind. Failing to do so may mean the force of rapid technological advancement runs roughshod over your organization, creating a number of problems along the way. These problems could grow in severity so quickly that the organization won't be able to effectively respond before their cash runs out.

The Future Leadership Framework will assist leaders with respect to the force of rapid technological advancement. Work that clarifies the organization's mission, sets the organization's strategy, and rebuffs the ability of technology to erode true leadership is all a part of this model. More on that framework is coming up in Part II of this book.

KEY IDEA

The force of rapid technological advancement describes the creep of ever-improving technology that has the potential to radically change what work is and how it gets done. As the technological curve continues skyward with each passing day, future leaders may have to change how they evaluate and implement new technology. Leaders no longer have the luxury of implementing potentially cost effective technology without considering the organization's mission. Nor can they overlook technological improvements simply due to their expense or complication. Technology implementation in the years ahead will require more thought and care than it does today.

5

Win the Future

LEVERAGE THE POWER OF LEADERSHIP

So far we have seen that the leadership effectiveness baseline is too low for too many organizations, and we have seen that these same organizations, already at a competitive disadvantage because of this underperforming leadership, are getting further stressed by the forces of generational churn and rapid technological advancement. Considering all of this, how can we win?

Leaders can win the future by fully leveraging the power of leadership. A lever is something that multiplies effort. Archimedes, the Greek mathematician, mentioned that with a lever long enough, the whole world could be moved. Leverage, for the sake of this book, is the ability of the future leader to direct their time, energy, and attention to activities that multiply their effort.

Creating leverage through leadership requires two actions. First, leaders will need to focus their time, energy, and attention on developing the lead domino skills that will best move other people to action on the organization's mission. Of all the skills a leader could choose to develop, the leader should focus on the skills that will improve the leadership effectiveness baseline, and best respond to the forces of generational churn and rapid technological advancement.

Second, as leaders develop these skills, they will need to spend more time on leadership activities and less time on technical activities than they might have in years past. Most leaders I know have a leadership component to their work and they have a technical component to their work. They are working leaders. But, to fully leverage the power of leadership within the same number of hours in a typical workday, these leaders will need to spend more time doing the work of leadership and less time doing their technical work. This may sound counterintuitive at first, but if we keep in mind that the work of leadership (when done correctly) multiplies effort, then it starts to make more sense. Ultimately, we want to invest more of our time on activities that multiply our effort instead of spending our time on things that don't.

I can already hear you protest because, if you are like others I have worked with, you don't feel there is enough time to do everything anyway, and now I am asking you to do more. But, let me nudge you a bit on this. You are right that there is not enough time to do any more. You are right to protest if you already feel overburdened. Most of us have reached the zenith of what we are able to cram into a single day. Since we can't do any more, the only other solution is to change what we do. To become leaders that effectively transition our organizations from today to tomorrow means we must rebalance how we allocate our time each day. I want you to strategically drop some things you spend your time on for other things you can invest in.

When we spend our time, it is gone. When we invest our time, we receive dividends later on.

To rebalance your time in this way means you will have to hear about it. It will likely create friction. Some people you work with won't like it. You might get sideways looks or unhelpful comments from your coworkers or managers. This happens with every change and it is unavoidable. But, I am way more interested in your success than keeping your coworkers' comments at bay. So, now that we know what to expect we can confidently move forward with the understanding that none of this will necessarily be easy, but it will be worth it.

We understand that we need to focus our time, energy, and attention on those skills that will raise both the leadership baseline and combat the forces of generational churn and rapid technological advancement. And, we also understand that to do this well means we must spend more time on leadership activities than other activities. To fully leverage leadership means we must invest in developing and deploying the skills found in a new leadership framework especially designed for the times. This framework I call the Future Leadership Framework.

As a future leader who deploys the Future Leadership Framework, you will use your time, energy, and attention to find, clearly define, and effectively communicate organizational goals in a way that inspires and motivates others. You will also develop and hone the interpersonal skills that will create an almost magnetic ability to attract and retain the most skilled talent. And, you will foster an environment where insane levels of productivity become an unremarkable norm.

We begin unpacking the Future Leadership Framework with the Creativity ability. Creativity, as it is applied in this framework, may not be what you expect.

Part II

THE FUTURE LEADERSHIP FRAMEWORK

6

CREATIVITY

THE FUTURE LEADER'S ABILITY TO CONTINUOUSLY FIND AND RESPOND TO THE RIGHT PROBLEMS

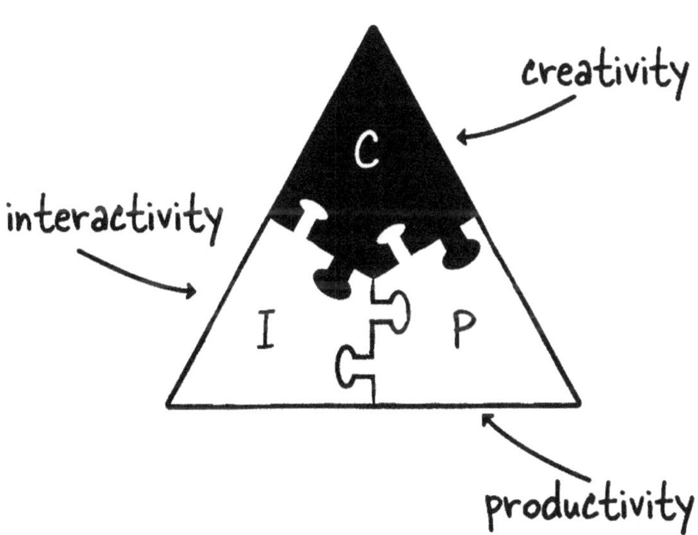

WHETHER THE ORGANIZATION is for profit or not-for-profit, one person or 40,000 people, the future leader who can continuously find and respond to the right problems despite an ever-accelerating and ambiguous business environment will provide their organization a better shot at success.

Creativity has been defined as the ability to transcend traditional ideas, rules, patterns, relationships, and to create meaningful new ideas, forms, methods, and interpretations.[1] Creativity is the first puzzle piece of the Future Leadership Framework.

For the future leader, this concept doesn't mean the same thing that it does for others in the organization. Technicians will use their hard skills and creativity to find new or innovative ways to solve problems the organization has already decided to solve. For the future leader, however, creativity is about finding the right problems to solve in the first place, and then organizing resources to tackle those problems.

There is no shortage of good opportunities vying for our time, energy, and attention. This problem will persist into the future and it will be compounded by the forces of generational churn and rapid technological advancement. Future leaders who embrace the skills found in this ability will be better poised to aim their organization's resources away from the merely good opportunities and toward those crucial few great opportunities.

The Creativity ability is a composition of three key skills:

1. Creating and communicating a mission that inspires and motivates;

2. Synthesizing mountains of data into stories the organization can act upon; and

3. Creating appropriate go-forward strategies.

We start with the fundamental skill of creating a mission that will light a fire under the people you work with.

7

Mission

FIND THE RIGHT PROBLEMS TO SOLVE

On May 25, 1961, President John F. Kennedy stood before a joint session of Congress and requested special funding for a project that has since set the benchmark for big, hairy, and audacious goals. At the time, the Russians were winning the space race and embarrassing the Americans. In October 1957, the United Soviet Socialist Republic launched Sputnik, the first satellite successfully put into Earth's orbit. Sputnik looked like a gray metal basketball with several straight antennae extending in a windswept arrangement behind the sphere.[1] Though this satellite weighed only 184 pounds and measured about 23 inches in diameter, it made a huge impact. The Russians were out in front and had a clear advantage. America needed to respond.

In front of that joint session of Congress, Kennedy described the impossible. "I believe that this nation should commit itself to achieving the goal, before this decade is out, of landing a man on the moon and returning him safely to the earth," he said.[2] Considering no American had yet left the atmosphere, this was a staggering pronouncement.

If we break this statement down, then Kennedy was proposing that America should put people inside of a spaceship that hasn't been built yet, rocket them out of Earth's atmosphere where they would complete several days of spaceflight, land on the moon which is 238,900 miles away, exit the spaceship on the moon to explore, rocket back off the surface of the moon, complete several more days of spaceflight back to Earth, and then land safely. And, by the way, this whole project should be completed in only nine years. President Kennedy set the literal moon shot goal.

The National Aeronautics and Space Administration (NASA), only three years old at the time of President Kennedy's speech, responded to the challenge. On July 24, 1969, 159 days before the deadline, Apollo 11 fulfilled Kennedy's goal.[3]

THE POWER OF A CLEARLY ARTICULATED MISSION

The power source for the goal as described above was not the money that Congress allocated to its completion. It wasn't the support it received from the American public. It wasn't even the technology itself. The primary power source was a clear mission. Having a clear and supported mission makes all the difference.

Imagine if President Kennedy had said, "I think we should make it a priority to investigate our moon." Not good. Murkiness always leads to confusion. What does "investigate" mean? What does "priority" mean (especially these days)? When should any of this get done? Instead, he made it clear what the expectation was and put a date on it. In return, NASA and the rest of the country responded, and Neil Armstrong became the first person to step foot on the moon.

Missions aren't reserved only for the exploration of space. Every organization and every team within an organization should create a clear and compelling mission as well. The mission of any organization represents a decision about what problems the organization has chosen to solve. The mission answers the question, "what is our purpose?" It is more than just what everybody does all day long—it is the intended outcome of all those actions combined.

Missions also aren't reserved for the organization as a whole. At the team level, leaders should create a mission that sets a clear and compelling purpose for the team. These sub-missions should align with the overall organizational mission.

Say you worked in a functionally divided organization in the accounting department. This accounting department would have its own mission that would in turn support the organization's overall mission. If you are a part of a cross-functional team, a mission would be developed to support whatever larger structure that team is a part of.

Super success at the organization level is a function of creating and aligning missions at the team or department level.

This notion might feel burdensome, but the future leader who focuses on it will be rewarded.

Finding teams that have created compelling missions is hard to do. Even finding compelling missions for organizations in

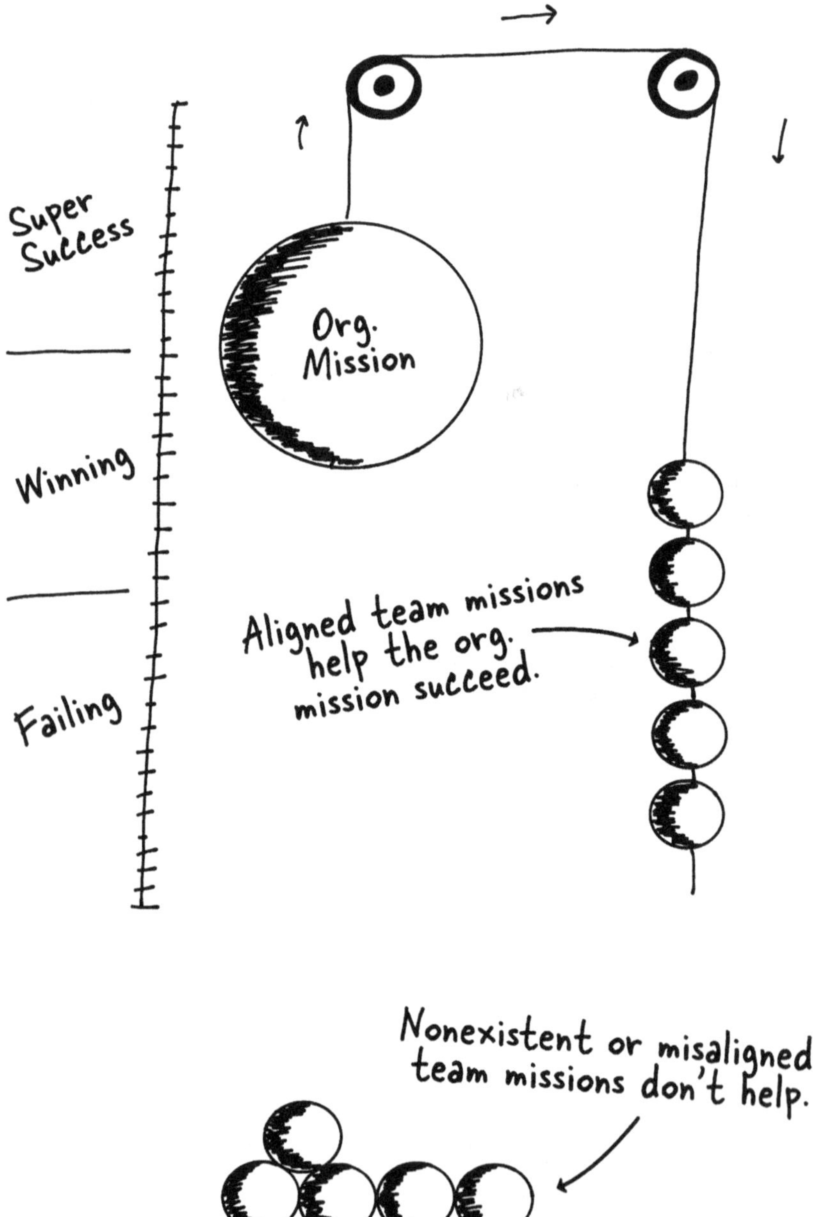
Super Success
Winning
Failing
Org. Mission
Aligned team missions help the org. mission succeed.
Nonexistent or misaligned team missions don't help.

general is becoming needle-in-the-haystack work. To be clear, we aren't necessarily talking about mission statements. Many organizations have mission statements, even though they are missing a compelling mission. The organizations, though, that have done the work to establish a compelling mission and then managed to articulate that mission in clear words have a definite advantage. Some examples of clear and compelling missions and their proper articulation come from ASOS, TED, and SpaceX.

Good Mission Example #1: ASOS Has a Clear and Compelling Mission

ASOS is in the business of selling clothes online. Their mission is to "become the world's number one online shopping destination for fashion-loving twenty-somethings."[4] This is one of the clearest, simplest, and most compelling missions I have come across. We know exactly what this company is trying to do. More importantly, ASOS employees know exactly what the company is trying to do.

Notice that ASOS uses clear language to describe its mission. No business buzzwords to be found. Notice how it uses a single sentence to describe their mission. By making the mission clear and tightly worded, they have made it much easier to remember.

Good Mission Example #2: How TED Spreads Ideas

TED is another example of an organization with a clear mission. TED is short for Technology Entertainment and Design, and is famous for creating the almost-verb-phrase "TED talk." A curated group of people are asked to present their ideas at a few large TED events each year and at several smaller TEDx events around the world. TED's mission is to "spread ideas."[5] To this end, you may be able to attend an in-person event for a fee, you can watch speakers online for free on YouTube, and you can listen to podcasts of these presentations. These avenues for watching or listening to a talk are the obvious way TED is spreading ideas. I would also argue that TED is helping to spread ideas in a much subtler way.

Spreading an idea is more complicated than it might appear on the surface. For an idea to effectively spread requires a few seemingly invisible steps. The idea has to be discovered, then polished, then adequately amplified. Only then does the idea have a chance to really spread.

TED FINDS THE GREAT IDEA. Great ideas are all around us, but not all of them see the light of day. In fact, relatively few do. One of TED's primary jobs is to find the great ideas in the first place. Ideas have to be found before they can be spread. Through their extended network and their established influence, TED event organizers can better find the people who have generated these ideas.

TED HELPS PREPARE THE IDEA. Once the idea is found, it usually has to make a journey from rough draft to final cut. TED presenters are generally experts in whatever they are talking about, but those in the audience may not be experts. Therefore, ideas need to be distilled into words and concepts that any audience can grasp. TED event organizers work with speakers to help them shape their great ideas into something that is ready for an audience. A poorly constructed great idea has a smaller chance of spreading than a well-constructed great idea.

TED AMPLIFIES THE IDEA. Even if you find a great idea and spend the time to construct it in a way that people can readily grasp, the idea still may not go anywhere without amplification. Some great and well-constructed ideas have never been adequately amplified and have therefore never spread as far as they could have. Amplification pushes the idea out to a large enough audience who can then share the idea with others.

In summary, for TED to fulfill its mission of spreading ideas, it must first find the raw, great ideas, then help people construct their raw, great ideas into a final draft form that any audience can understand, and then adequately amplify the finished idea. The mission of TED isn't to slap a conference together, have a few people drop by to read their PowerPoint slides, and then broadcast the result online. That arrangement would have a smaller chance of effectively spreading ideas. TED takes an altogether different approach, and as a result, they are able to fulfill their mission and "spread (great) ideas" to millions of people each year.

Good Mission Example #3: SpaceX and the Long Game

SpaceX is in the business of more economically putting things into space. This fifteen-year-old commercial space company, run by Elon Musk, is "the world's fastest-growing provider of launch services and has over 70 future missions on its manifest representing over $10 billion in contracts."[6] SpaceX has a clear mission and purpose for its existence. Its mission is to "design, manufacture, and launch advanced rockets and spacecraft ... with the ultimate goal of enabling people to live on other planets."[7]

Enabling people to live on other planets is a big deal. It is more of a stretch than the first moon landing. Fulfilling this mission will take years of dedicated focus. The people at SpaceX have difficult technical problems to solve before it becomes feasible to live on Mars. SpaceX is playing the long game when it comes to their mission. It has established what it's trying to do and is working backwards to make that vision a reality. While the ultimate goal might be decades away, imagine how motivating it would be to work for a place with a crystal clear vision and mission.

MISSION AS DECISION-MAKING FRAMEWORK

I chose these three companies as case studies because their missions illustrate a fundamental concept. Effective missions serve not only to inspire and motivate the people who work for the company, but also provide a framework for decision-making. Missions help leaders figure out which problems their organizations should focus on solving.

ASOS aims to be number one with fashion-loving twenty-somethings, which means they are setting aside work on forty-somethings' fashion trends. TED is not in the business of creating ideas. Their mission is to spread ideas. The mission of SpaceX isn't solely to create rocket technology. They are trying to make interplanetary travel and living a reality.

Clear missions like these aren't common. More common are missions with four basic mistakes. These mistakes put organizations at a distinct disadvantage in attracting and retaining all generations of skilled workers, and implementing advancing technology appropriately.

Mistake #1: The Organization Failed to Create a Mission in the First Place

The first mistake happens when an organization fails to create a mission. There is no rule that says an organization must have a mission, and some organizations choose to be mission-free. Organizations that are mission-free can continue operating year after year, and they might even be consistently profitable, but they always lack direction. They are wandering in the woods.

These organizations aren't sure what to focus on and what to set aside. They aren't sure where to deploy resources and what resources should be reallocated. They struggle to find success because they haven't defined what success is. The people who work in these organizations are unable to connect the work they do each day with a larger purpose. They know what the work is, but not why any of it matters. When an organization is mission-free, its employees are often motivation-free.

Mistake #2: The Organization Has a Mission Statement but No Actual Mission

Organizations that have mission statements without clearly defined missions are similar to organizations that don't have a mission at all. They can't align work and resources with a larger purpose because they have not clearly articulated the larger purpose with which they need to align. They might have a nice plaque on the wall that is filled with business buzzwords that sound good, but they make little attempt to act on the words.

These organizations tend to have teams with diffused effort. Without the clarity of a real mission, every idea becomes a potentially good idea worthy of being acted on. Leaders take on the task of green-lighting or red-lighting projects from a place of weakness rather than a place of strength because there is no fundamental decision-making framework in place.

Based on their mission, one can infer that if a team at ASOS made a pitch for a new project that was sure to capture some niche in the fifty-something market, they would be instantly shut down. ASOS has made it clear that they are about serving twenty-somethings. However, if ASOS had a nice plaque on the wall without the discipline to align their actions to the mission, then this pitch for serving fifty-somethings might have better luck. The result would be a watering down of ASOS' influence in their particular niche.

Mistake #3: The Organization Has a Strong Mission but Weak Implementation

This is what happens when organizations fail to give a hard "no" and instead give a sheepish "yes." People can feel whether there is true support behind an initiative. The riskier the initiative is, the more this support matters. But, some organizations have leadership that just can't say no.

Being mission-oriented requires future leaders to have the courage to turn down potential new initiatives because they are out of alignment. Future leaders have to be prepared to turn down these initiatives even if they might be lucrative in the short run. These leaders can turn down these misaligned initiatives because they know they have to preserve time, energy, and attention for other initiatives that are aligned with the mission.

For the future organization, having a clear and compelling mission assumes a new level of importance. There should not be a single decision made inside an organization where somebody isn't asking, "How does this serve our mission?" Everything should be viewed through this lens. Every meeting, every office supply order, every newly proposed team, every office party, every technology purchase, every hire, every expenditure, and every new client acquisition strategy should be routed through this basic decision-making framework.

Mistake #4: The Organization's Leadership Fails to Communicate the Mission

We saw an earlier statistic that more than two-thirds of people can't tell you what the mission of their organization is.[8] This is likely the case because the mission hasn't been communicated often enough or in a sticky enough way. Leaders should feel like politicians on the stump when it comes to their mission. Ideas take a while to settle in.

The Role of the Mission

The purpose of any organization is to manifest an outcome in the world. The mission, whether it's written down as a formal mission statement or not, serves to clarify what that outcome is. In this way, an organization's mission serves as the basic decision-making framework that helps the organization's leaders determine how to allocate scarce resources. The other role a mission has is to inspire and motivate the people who are working in the organization and the people who are investing in it. Do right by your organization and by your team, and create a clear and compelling mission.

Beyond my feelings about the importance of mission, the data shows that mission-driven organizations consistently outperform their counterparts. Mission-driven organizations have much higher levels of innovation and engagement and tend to be first or second in their market segment.[9] Clear and compelling missions aren't about corporate "Kumbaya," rather they directly translate into better financial performance.

CREATING A CLEAR AND COMPELLING MISSION

Creating a clear and compelling mission at the organizational level or team level is really about finding the right problems to solve in the first place. Finding the right problems to solve in a quickly changing business landscape requires the future leader's time and attention.

The research indicates that only about one-third of Millennials feel strongly connected to their company's mission.[10] As the workplace makes its epic transition from Baby Boomers to Millennials, what problems the organization intends to solve may also need to transition. Just because the organization has been solving one set of problems for the past twenty years, doesn't mean those problems will continue to be the right ones to solve.

For the future leader, figuring out which problem or problems to solve is a big deal. With so much change in the workplace, it will become easier to chase after bright and shiny objects in lieu of making dedicated progress on the right problems. The bright and shiny object syndrome is exacerbated by new technologies that open doors to other possibilities.

To better keep your organization on track, here are some ideas that will help.

BE BRAVE. Creating a mission is an act of bravery in two respects. When you create your mission, you will choose where to focus the organization's or your team's assets, and by default, you will choose where not to focus. The first act of bravery happens when those decisions are made as the mission is formed. The second act of bravery happens when the organization or the team turns away potential revenue because the client or the project does not align with the mission. This is hard to do, especially when future leaders have to turn down potentially lucrative, but misaligned, initiatives.

GET NECESSARY BUY-IN. Missions should not be created by a single individual in a corner cubicle and then bestowed upon the rest of the staff. That won't elicit the necessary buy-in that all missions require. The act of creating or editing a mission should be done with as many people as possible. All team members should participate. Large organizations should have a healthy cross-section of their employees represented. Missions that go on to become the initial decision-making framework will require people who are bought in. Buy-in comes, in part, when people feel they have a stake in the process and the outcome.

CREATE EXAMPLE STORIES. The words on the wall might be the words that describe your mission, but all great missions have stories that help to illustrate them. What are the stories attached to your organization's mission? Dig for a few stories about customers you helped that illustrates your mission in action. Take the time to shape those stories into something memorable and then frequently share those stories with the staff and with investors.

COMMUNICATE THE MISSION FREQUENTLY. Future leaders should have the missions of their organization and their teams embedded in their souls. It's not about drinking the organizational Kool-Aid, but about communicating the mission enough so others really understand it. You might become tired of repeating it, but I assure you that somebody you work with is just now getting it. The stories that you create and communicate around the mission will help the information stick.

REVIEW THE MISSION REGULARLY. Missions are not "set it and forget it." These are living sentiments that need regular attention. Future leaders should expect to review the organization's mission each quarter and ask themselves: Does the mission still hold in its current form? Has the market or the wider ecosystem changed? Are we still solving the right problems? What are customers and staff saying? Talk over these observations with others. Don't treat missions as cast in stone, because they aren't. Be fluid and flexible in your approach.

SAY NO, OFTEN. The true power of missions come from the power they give future leaders to say no. If the initiative *du jour* doesn't align, you have a way out. Blame the mission. "Sorry, this doesn't align well enough with our mission." Saying no to the activities that are outside of the mission means that you preserve time, energy, and attention for the problems that better align with the mission.

LAST WORD ON MISSION

In the Future Leadership Framework, finding the right problems to solve is one of the essential skills future leaders will need to hone. Organizations are essentially problem-solving machines. But what problems should be solved? For the future leader dealing with generational churn in the workplace coupled with rapid technological advancement, finding the right problems to solve becomes even more important. Effective missions serve as a decision-making framework in addition to inspiring and motivating workers.

KEY IDEA

Right now, the evidence shows that a number of organizations don't do enough when it comes to developing or communicating their missions. Taking the time to hone and communicate the mission will help keep future generations engaged at work. Also, a clear and compelling mission will help future leaders respond to the force of rapid technological advancement by providing a way to evaluate new technologies against the organization's basic purpose.

KEY DIFFERENCES

Yesterday's Leader

Creates confusing mission statements
Doesn't communicate the mission
Doesn't use mission for decision-making

The Future Leader

Creates a clear mission
Communicates it often and with stories
Uses the mission for decision-making

KEY QUESTION

Can you clearly and succinctly articulate the missions of your organization and your team?

8

Synthesis

CREATE STORIES FROM DATA

A FEW YEARS AGO, I interviewed the owner of a company that operated commercial drones. He told me about how farmers in eastern Washington State used his drones to help manage their acreage. "What does this do for the farmers?" I asked. He provided a long-winded answer that could be summed up as, "It provides them with better data about their farms."

I drilled down a bit deeper. "What kind of data do the drones collect, and how does it help the farmers?" He explained how a drone equipped with special sensing equipment could systematically analyze the conditions of a farm and report back on a number of farm metrics. The data coming in included soil-moisture levels, crop density, weed and disease conditions, yield estimates, and more. For a few dollars per acre and a time investment of a day or two, the farmer would receive a number of data points about the farm. With these data points, the farmer could alter watering patterns or frequencies, or the distribution of fertilizer. The data could also help the farmer optimize heavy equipment operations, and provide the farmer better information about the expected crop yield ahead of harvest.

All of these data points help the farmer decide which potential actions would best optimize the farm. An optimized farm produces the highest crop yield for the lowest marginal cost. For the farmer, turning the data into actionable information improves the business of farming.

TURNING DISPARATE DATA POINTS INTO STORIES

Data can help farmers farm, and data can help your organization better fulfill its mission. Data itself, though, is worthless without somebody, or something, to analyze that data and turn it into actionable information.

The process of turning disparate bits of data into actionable information, or what I call "stories," is the skill of Synthesis.

Creating stories out of data isn't always easy. In the farmer example, we can better understand why this might be the case. After the drone flights are done and the farmer has received the report, the farmer has to connect a variety of dots before taking action.

Imagine this scenario: The farmer receives a drone report noting that several acres in a portion of the farm are drier than they should be and drier than the acreage around it. The farmer could quickly turn this data into a story that he should increase the amount of water in this area, but is this story right? Before turning up the water flow—an expensive response to a story—the farmer decides to look at last year's drone flight to compare the conditions.

Last year's report notes that this section was just as moist as the surrounding acreage. Now the farmer has more data that creates an alternative story. It may not be that watering needs to be increased, but that the watering machines have some sort of mechanical problem preventing them from watering this section of acreage appropriately. With this new story, the farmer can now consider a different course of action.

The process of finding the right data and then turning that data into stories that can be acted upon represents a fundamental skill that future leaders will need to master. The problem is, this process is getting much harder to do as the amount of data available to create stories from grows exponentially.

Internal Data Is Growing Exponentially

A recent check of the Real Time Statistics Project website revealed that almost 2.7 million email messages were sent in one second.[1] There were already more than 1.2 million blog posts posted on the morning I checked the site. Over 17 million photos were already uploaded to Instagram. Websites were being added to the internet every second with over 1.2 billion sites put up so far. While these data points may not be important to your organization, they are a good representation of the amount of data we are generating. EMC reports that 44 zettabytes of data will be generated each year by 2020.[2] That's 44 trillion gigabytes of data each year! To put this number into perspective, 16 gigabytes of data will be generated every day for each person alive on Earth.

We walked through a small data example with the farmer already, but what about big data? Big data is a big deal for large organizations. Take Amazon, for example. Think about the potential data generated by the last Amazon purchase you made. Amazon knows what you bought. It knows how much you paid for it, what time it was purchased, where it is being shipped to, and how you paid for it. It knows what other products you looked at before buying the one you settled one. It knows if you read questions associated with the product and, if so, what questions. It knows if you read reviews and if you marked any reviews helpful, and if you watched a product video on the site or not. It knows what browser you used to surf their site or whether you used a mobile app. The point is, there are almost more potential data points available than can be reasonably collected from just a single sale on Amazon's platform.

Now, imagine the number of data points that could be generated from a single sale and multiply this number by the number of items Amazon sells in a given day. Better yet, imagine how much data could be generated on a special sale day like Prime Day. It was estimated that more than 600 items were sold every second during Prime Day 2016 (almost 52 million items).[3] For Prime Day 2017, Amazon's sales jumped another 60 percent over the 2016 numbers.[4] The data coming in from these transactions is where the term "big data" comes from.

A number of organizations are jumping on the data-collection bandwagon. In one survey of several hundred companies, 30 percent of respondents had undertaken a big-data project (up from 20 percent two years earlier).[5] The trend is leaning toward the collection and attempted synthesis of ever-growing data sets. And, this voluminous data will continue to exponentially increase as the Internet of Things continues its expansion.

The Internet of Things—objects that can exchange data, like light bulbs that can be controlled by Amazon's Alexa, or autonomous cars that can drive you to work—adds to the data explosion. Intel estimates that by 2020, there will be 200 billion connected objects around the world, up from just 2 billion objects in 2006.[6] For the future leader leading the future organization, just wrapping their minds around the data will be difficult to do, let alone turning that data into stories that influence next actions.

And, External Data Is Growing Exponentially

Big data does not only come from internal business transactions. In an intensely networked, globalizing economy, data also flows readily from sources outside of the organization. Larger geopolitical trends happening somewhere in the world can now appreciably affect an organization operating in a different part of the world. Data coming in about the health of, and opportunities within, the industry that the organization operates in also need to be converted into stories that will inform future actions. The future leader will not only be responsible for synthesizing data from product or service sales, but will also be responsible for collecting and synthesizing data being generated from the wider ecosystem.

SYNTHESIS BECOMES EVEN MORE IMPORTANT

Creating stories from data is a required skill of the future leader. Why? According to McKinsey, "data-driven organizations are twenty-three times more likely to acquire customers, six times as likely to retain those customers, and nineteen times as likely to be profitable as a result."[7] All organizations stand to benefit from optimization that comes from using data to create stories that inform future actions.

The problem is that just as the need for this skill is increasing, our collective ability to properly analyze data and turn it into stories is being undermined. This is partly a people problem, and partly a technology problem. Let's start with people.

Will Future Generations Have Fewer Analytical Skills?

Just as there are preferential differences among the generations, so too are there skill differences. This makes sense as the people who make up the generations have a different level of experience in the workplace and in life. One common refrain is that Millennials are lacking in analytical skills, for instance.

A finding from a survey sponsored by the American Management Association that included over 800 respondents from 50 different industries showed that Millennials were rated the lowest in analytical strength. Respondents noted that almost 20 percent of Millennials are perceived to have fewer analytical skills as compared to other generations.[8] Other data collected by the Program for the International Assessment of Adult Competencies was analyzed by the assessment company ETS. What ETS found was that 50 percent of US Millennials were not proficient at applying math and reading skills at work.[9]

The skill of Synthesis relies heavily on reading comprehension and mathematical skills. In the world of work we aren't given discreet equations to solve. Instead, every problem is story problem waiting to be solved by those with the right skills. If members of the largest generation ever to occupy the workplace have a problem with their analytical capabilities, this is a serious problem for future leaders. Not only will the skill of Synthesis become important to personally develop, but it will become increasingly important to help develop this skill in future generations as well.

Synthesis Is Being Undermined by Technological Advance

The people part of the problem is only half of this equation. Technological advancements are also working to undermine the skill of Synthesis. Patricia Greenfield, a professor of psychology at UCLA, notes that an inverse relationship exists between technology and our ability to critically think. Specifically, tech has improved our visual skills, but our critical thinking and analysis skills have decreased.[10]

Critical thinking and analysis skills are not inherent skills for any of us. They are skills that we develop and hone over time. As more of us lean on the crutch of technology to answer our questions, our ability to analyze the essence of any question, and then evaluate potential solutions with that essence in mind, can diminish. A Google search might be able to give you an answer, but it cannot (yet) put any answer into context. Context is key, and our ability to accurately synthesize data comes from understanding the context surrounding the data. Questions and their associated answers out of context don't have enough heft to be useful. With the rise of AI, this problem of crutch-leaning will surely continue.

IMPROVING THE SKILL OF SYNTHESIS

The Future Leadership Framework requires mastering the skill of Synthesis. This skill will not only help to optimize the sales of the products and services your organization already offers, but will also help inform the mission of the organization. The multitude of ways a future leader can synthesize information is a secondary concern. The Future Leadership Framework stresses creating the right model, and then employing the right tactics to create the stories that inform next actions. This is why the skill of Synthesis is part of the Creativity ability. The following are a few key ideas to assist future leaders in developing this skill.

GET CLEAR ON THE "WHAT." What are you trying to do with the data? Is this about improving sales? Is this about improving customer service? Is this about market research for a new product or service? Don't start with the data and move forward—start with what you are trying to accomplish and move backward. Write down what you are trying to do so you and your team are clear. Spend some time with this question about what to do with the data to make sure you are asking the right questions. Data has a sneaky way of making any ill-defined objective more confusing, which is why we want to start with clarity.

IDENTIFY WHAT DATA IS NEEDED. Defining the end goal will determine where you need to collect the data from. If your organization is analyzing sales numbers for potential improvement, then collecting and evaluating data that is generated prior to the sale and after the sale may be just as valuable as data from the sale itself. If your organization is analyzing its customer service program for potential improvement, then it may make sense to start collecting customer survey data about their experience with your organization in addition to other data. The point here is that your goal will help inform what data needs to be collected.

BE RESULTS AGNOSTIC. Now that the team knows what the objective is, it is time to review the data. Remember the original television show *CSI: Crime Scene Investigation*? Gil Grissom, played by William Petersen, would say, "We have to follow the evidence." The future leader will need to create their own results-agnostic posture just as Grissom did. The problem is that with so much data available, there will be ample opportunity to focus only on data that supports a preconceived idea. We like to be right. Future leaders will need to be self-effacing enough to shift the emphasis from who is right to what is right.

REGULARLY PULL BACK. Future leaders need to regularly return their gaze to the horizon. Sometimes the problem with data is that it can suck you down into the weeds. At regular intervals, pull back and look at where the team is. Are you still moving in the right direction? Are you getting closer to creating stories that can be acted upon?

CHALLENGE ASSUMPTIONS. Statisticians have a saying: correlation is not causation. Just because two variables moved at the same time doesn't mean one influenced the other. A snowy winter on the East Coast and a warm, wet winter on the West Coast may be correlated, but one is not causing the other. As you and your team create stories from the data, make sure to challenge the assumptions that undergird the stories. These assumptions come from the data but also come from our innate biases. Ask questions. Be methodical. What else could be influencing the story the data points are creating? What less obvious or hidden factors may be contributing?

GET OUTSIDE OPINIONS EARLY AND OFTEN. Working with others to create the stories from the data is a way to challenge assumptions and ask for alternate opinions. Just because you are interpreting data one way, doesn't mean that is the only way it could be interpreted. Get another set of eyes to look at the data. Do this early in the process. The most successful future leaders will set up systems of outside review that ensure the stories they are creating are also stress-tested by outside analysis.

KEEP FOCUSED ON THE END GOAL. The end goal of synthesis is not to create stories for the sake of stories. The ultimate goal is to implement the right actions because of the stories. The stories that come from the data are what will move others to action, so these stories need to be as accurate as possible. As we pull together disparate bits of data, especially when it gets tough, remembering the overall goal will help us cross the finish line.

EMBRACE UNCERTAINTY. Because our information will continue to be incomplete, our stories will never be as complete or as convincing as they could be. Part of being a future leader is working through uncomfortable uncertainty. From now on we simply won't have all the information. Partly, this is because there is so much information to begin with, and partly it's because the information is subject to change on a frequent basis. Getting comfortable creating stories from incomplete information will be key in the years ahead.

USE SYNTHESIS WIDELY. We can use the essential skill of Synthesis in all areas of our work. We will be able to improve internal business processes, or even our own work processes. The ability to examine data and turn it into stories to act upon should inform all aspects of our work.

USING RAPID TECHNOLOGICAL ADVANCEMENT AS AN ADVANTAGE

Technology is responsible for much of the data we are swimming in. It's not that the data wasn't being generated all along, but now we have the ability to collect, sort, and store it fairly easily. The data baggage that has come with widespread technological adoption has helped organizations move from anecdotes and intuition to informed decision-making. And, as technology continues to advance, the skill of Synthesis will become even more important.

Data that is still too painful to collect or organize will be collected and organized in the years ahead. Organizations will have more data on who uses their products and services, how they use those products and services, and why they made their particular choices. Organizations will also have better information on the external trends that may affect their operations.

I see a trend emerging in which collecting data will become easier, while synthesizing the data "by hand" will become harder. The answer: employ better technology to help with some of the heavy lifting. Engineers are already designing machine learning and AI programs to help turn data into actionable information at scale. At MetLife, for instance, the blend of data and AI is improving customer service by helping to process claims much faster and at a lower cost.[11] MetLife is using AI to quickly turn patient data into stories they can act on.

The ability to merge available data with AI to create useful stories won't be solely for big companies like MetLife. The ability to borrow the technology to aid in synthesis is already a reality. IBM's Watson is now available over the internet for companies to use. As IBM reports, "…in 45 countries and 20 industries, people are working with Watson to help make better decisions and make their best work better."[12] Amazon offers machine learning and AI through its Amazon Web Services program. As better AI gets developed, and in platforms that smaller businesses can more readily access, the ability to synthesize data will become much easier.

Amid this, it can be confusing to understand what role the future leader plays. AI may help synthesize the data much faster, but ultimately people will determine which stories should be acted upon. AI may increase the speed of story creation, but it will still be incumbent on the future leader to make the final informed decision. The need for the skill of Synthesis becomes more important, not less, because of better technology.

Synthesis for the future leader, as a result, will necessarily be fluid, and will require these leaders to assume different roles in making data-driven decisions. The future leader may have the role of creating the systems to capture and collect the data, or the role of synthesizing the data into stories, or the role of reviewing the analysis and synthesis of the AI, or some combination of these roles.

LAST WORD ON SYNTHESIS

In the farther future, mountains of seemingly disparate bits of data will be collected, analyzed, and turned into actionable stories by complex AI programs for ultimate review by humans. Some organizations may be in a position where they are comfortable opting to skip the human review part depending on the type of decisions being made and the robustness of the AI. The skill of Synthesis will never go away, however. Future leaders will always have a role at some level when it comes to taking action based on the stories created from the data.

KEY IDEA

Synthesis is the process of converting data into actionable information, or stories, that can then be used by organizations to guide potential actions. Synthesis is a key skill in the Future Leadership Framework because the value to the organization of making data-driven decisions will only increase in the years ahead.

KEY DIFFERENCES

Yesterday's Leader

Creates stories from intuition
Doesn't take the time to create stories
Often gets narrow in data analysis

The Future Leader

Creates stories from data
Creates stories to guide actions
Goes wide in data analysis

KEY QUESTION

Do you regularly make data-driven decisions, or do you tend to make decisions based off intuition?

9

Strategy

SET THE ORGANIZATION'S SAIL

IN 2008, TROUBLE WAS brewing for Starbucks, and Howard Schultz could see it coming. The 2007 memo sent from Schultz as Chairman of the Board to CEO Jim Donald made a compelling case.[1] Schultz's view was that an accumulation of small decisions was moving Starbucks in the wrong direction. The memo, meant for an internal audience, was soon posted online and became the memo read 'round the world.

The growth strategy the company was using at the time, as described by Schultz, "led to the watering-down of the Starbucks experience, and, what some might call the 'commoditization' of our brand."[2] Schultz's observation was that a number of decisions the company made were probably right at the time, but in sum were problematic. Among other things, the strategy that Starbucks employed in the years ahead of the memo succeeded in opening a number of new stores—Starbucks opened an average of almost 1,900 new stores per year in the five years before Schultz's memo—but the strategy had the unintended effect of diluting the Starbucks experience. Over time, the rapid rate of expansion coupled with the compounding of small decisions had taken its toll.

As the financial markets continued to recede in what would

later be termed the "Great Recession," Starbucks found itself in a kind of trouble that can only be fully appreciated in hindsight. The Starbucks we know and love today is the same Starbucks whose future was as uncertain as the financial markets were in 2008.

As the broader economy was melting down in 2008, Schultz returned to the CEO role in an effort to right the ship. When Starbucks stock bottomed out at about four dollars per share in November 2008, Schultz illustrated how bad their situation was: "the problems were so severe, and every rock that I turned over was worse than I had imagined—to the point where I made some very drastic decisions."[3]

Starbucks had the pieces it needed. It had the stores. It had talented partners (employees) staffing those stores. It had its supply chain figured out. But it needed a new way to edit and organize those pieces so the company could return to its vision and prepare for the future.

THE STARBUCKS STRATEGY

Schultz talked about making drastic decisions. "Decisions" in this case refers to strategy. In essence, the company needed to go from where it was in the last half of 2008 to a future that is the company's reality today, with 25,000 stores and a stock price north of $50 per share.[4]

Since the company was in the special kind of trouble that happens when internal problems get magnified by an economy that is essentially falling apart, Schultz's strategy had to be bold. To illustrate how bold, let's look at a few of the larger components of the strategy Schultz ultimately deployed.

Strategy Component #1: Footprint

One component of Starbucks' new strategy was to be more intentional about its footprint. Up until this time, Starbucks had been aggressively opening new stores. In a short time after Schultz's return, Starbucks ended up closing several hundred newer and unprofitable stores. Schultz noted that the company ended up shuttering 900 stores during that time, 90 percent of which had been open for less than a year.[5]

This was a big move for Starbucks. At the end of fiscal 2008, Starbucks had 16,680 stores worldwide with 7,238 stores located in the United States.[6] Closing 900 locations meant the company shaved about 12 percent of their stores. In addition to closing stores, Starbucks also drastically slowed the rate of new store openings. From 2008 through 2011, the company only opened a few hundred additional stores.[7] Getting intentional about its footprint was a very visible and strong signal to the financial markets, Starbucks' customers, and their partners that the company was responding to its problems.

Strategy Component #2: Retraining

Another component of Starbucks' strategy was its massive retraining initiative. On February 26, 2008, Starbucks closed every United States company-owned store for over three hours. During that evening 135,000 Starbucks employees would undergo retraining in an effort to "renew focus on espresso standards."[8] A Starbucks spokesperson said, "They will be trained in creating the perfect shot, steaming the milk, and all the pieces that come together in a drink."[9] Echoing the theme of Schultz's memo, the spokesperson added, "It's really about ensuring that the customer experience that we provide is the best that it can be."[10]

This was huge. Just at the time when the company was in serious financial trouble, its leadership made a dramatic move to shoulder the costs of the retraining effort and the lost sales as a result of the temporary store closures. Why would Starbucks do this? Was the problem really that the baristas had forgotten how to prepare a proper latte? What about the sales that Starbucks would lose from this massive one-time closure?

Said Schultz, "We believe this is a bold demonstration of our commitment to our core and a reaffirmation of our coffee leadership."[11] This strategy component sent another strong signal to the financial markets, Starbucks' customers, and partners.

Strategy Component #3: Conference

A third component of the strategy was hosting the North American Leadership Conference. In 2008, Starbucks hosted 10,000 store managers in New Orleans. As Schultz noted, "We believe that this is the most important and strategic event that we can hold for our store managers and above, because this is another way to build understanding of our vision and strategy, as well as connect and help continue career development."[12]

Schultz was essentially using this event to return employees at all Starbucks stores to the same page. Just as closing the company stores for retraining was a big and costly move, so too was hosting this leadership conference, which was reported to cost $30 million.[13]

The strategy that Starbucks settled on and implemented was informed by the conditions both inside and outside the company. The strategy sought to reverse some internal decisions—like removing "stinky" breakfast sandwiches—while responding to broader problems caused by worsening economic conditions.

Similarly, the business conditions inside and outside other organizations will inform their strategy. It will be up to future leaders to create strategies considering these conditions. The difference for future leaders is that creating strategy in the years ahead must take into account all of the normal influences on the organization in addition to the forces of generational churn and rapid technological advancement.

STRATEGY FOR FUTURE LEADERS

A large sailboat is docked in the harbor and the crew is looking to reposition the boat to another harbor across a vast bay. It is a beautiful, sunny day and the wind is blowing steadily across the water. The crew looks at the conditions as they prepare to depart and notice that the winds are not favorable, but they aren't bad enough to call off the trip.

While underway, an experienced captain monitors the boat's course. The winds have shifted somewhat, and a straight shot across the bay is not feasible. Now they must tack the vessel into the wind at different angles to make it across. The captain sets the sail in the appropriate position to maximize their forward progress, considering their ultimate destination and the shifting winds. While they aren't following the shortest route across water, they are moving at maximum efficiency.

The sailboat is your organization and the captain is the future leader. The organization has a starting point and the organization has a goal. Now it needs a plan to move from the starting point to the goal. This plan is the strategy. Strategies are informed by the "winds" that are influencing the organization. Using the winds inefficiently or ignoring the winds altogether means you risk capsizing the organization on one extreme, or you risk allowing the organization to stall on the other.

Today's organizations are experiencing radically shifting winds. The shift is coming from a number of factors that tend to affect organizations all the time, but the shift is also a direct result of the forces of generational churn and rapid technological advancement.

Shifting Winds: The Generations

We looked at this earlier, but it's worth emphasizing again the significant level of change that will happen in organizations over the next few years as Baby Boomers continue to retire and the Millennials continue to migrate in and up the organization. Whatever strategies organizations conceive, effective implementation will depend, in part, on who will execute them. Old and bloated strategies foisted upon future generations may not receive the buy-in required to make them successful. Future leaders will need to create strategies with the wind of future generations in mind.

Shifting Winds: Technology

Imagine that one of your competitors creates a product similar to what your organization offers but has invested in automation such that they are able to cut production costs by 15 percent. If your response is to maintain the current set of the sail—to not change anything—then you will likely fall behind. To avoid falling behind, you will also need to reset your organization's sail according to the shifting winds.

The challenge for future leaders is that potentially disruptive technology is accelerating. In essence, the winds will shift more radically in the years ahead.

Dynamic Strategy

Dynamism in this sense should be equated to strategy that is light and flexible. Heavy strategy will take too much energy to create and too much energy to change. Heavy strategy could act as an anchor that holds your organization in place. With that in mind, I am still a fan of creating strategic plans, just lighter and more focused ones. I hesitate to use the term "strategic plan" because I can already feel your eyes rolling from here.

One article on strategic planning notes that, "executives at most companies criticize it as overly bureaucratic, insufficiently insightful, and ill-suited for today's rapidly changing markets."[14] Would you agree? I agree that traditional strategic plans of yesteryear won't have a home in the future organization. Things are moving too fast to spend an onerous amount of time meeting with a cross-section of organizational teams and consultants to create a formal strategic plan.

So, why not think of these plans differently? What if they weren't complex and what if they were geared for the new short term instead of the long term? What if the whole plan could be captured in just a few pages? A clear strategic direction is important. A heavy strategic plan is not.

Key Performance Indicators

Strategies by their very construction are usually vague. The problem with anything that is vague is that a gap is created between understanding what the strategy is and defining appropriate action. The gap can further manifest when daily actions delink from the broader strategy.

To help link actions to the strategies, there has to be a middleman of sorts. The middleman in this case is the key performance indicator. Key performance indicators are the concrete and easy to understand metrics that demonstrate progress. Key performance indicators serve to focus organizational action.

Any one strategy may have a number of corresponding key performance indicators. When done correctly, these key performance indicators will influence the daily work at the organization. When done incorrectly, people end up doing work that is not aligned with the key performance indicators, which then thwarts progress toward the strategy. Let's look at an example for context.

If one of your strategies was to "use speaking engagements to increase consulting sales," then a key performance indicator might be any of the following:

1. Number of association or chamber of commerce speaking engagements solicited each month;

2. Number of speaking gigs booked for associations or chambers of commerce each quarter;

3. Number of leads generated from each speaking event;

4. Number of consulting conversions from each event; or

5. Ratio of consulting conversions from each lead.

The idea is to break down vague strategy statements into metrics that can be measured. Only by measuring progress can that strategy be properly evaluated for its overall impact on the mission.

IMPROVING THE SKILL OF STRATEGY

Strategy in and of itself isn't a problem, but the manner in which we go about thinking and developing strategies that will create advantages for our organizations must adapt to the changing times. Some ideas:

EMBRACE THE CASCADE. The guiding statements of an organization should be aligned such that they create a cascade. The cascade starts with an organization's **belief**, which in turn informs the **vision**, which informs the **mission**, which informs the **strategies,** which inform the **key performance indicators**, which *should* inform your team's **focus** each week. It is all tied together. When all of these are in alignment, an organization creates more leverage with the resources it already has. This leverage comes from clarity and focus.

REMEMBER THAT STRATEGIES ARE FOR ORGANIZATIONS *AND* TEAMS. We said earlier that each organization should have a mission, and each team within the organization should have a supporting mission. Any time there is a mission, the organization needs to create strategies for achieving that mission. So, not only should there be organization-wide strategies, but there should be strategies created at the team level. If you are a team leader, you have the ultimate responsibility for creating and aligning the team's mission and strategies. This will provide perspective and clarity to the work that the team is focused on each day.

GET CLEAR ON WHERE YOU ARE. What harbor are you starting from? It is impossible to know where you want to end up until you have a clear picture of where you are starting. Is your mission clear, compelling, and actionable? Where are you succeeding and where has there been less success? Consider performing a SWOT analysis—Strengths, Weaknesses, Opportunities, and Threats. Be as detailed and as granular as possible.

GET CLEAR ON WHERE YOU WANT TO BE. Just as you need to be clear on where the organization is starting from, you will also need to be clear on where the finish line is. What does success look like? Be as detailed as possible so everybody understands. The ideal strategy in a strategic plan is clear, concise, uses plain words, and is constructed in a way that others can instantly understand. Attach numbers, percentages, dates, or anything else to assist in keeping the strategy as clear as possible. Be careful not to think about any finish line as the end. Once you reach the finish line, then it's time to create another finish line to work toward.

EVALUATE YOUR RESOURCES. What resources do you have that will help you go from one harbor to another? Yes, you have people who can help execute on the strategies. Yes, you might have a budget to help execute on the strategies. Do you have buy-in on the strategies from the people who will be implementing the work? Do your people have enough time and bandwidth in their day for work that supports a new metric or strategy? Defining what resources are actually available will inform whether the strategies you are contemplating are realistic.

CREATE KEY PERFORMANCE INDICATORS. From the cascade mentioned above, organizations, or teams within organizations, should create key performance indicators for the strategies that are adopted. The key performance indicators further break down a strategy into metrics that can be measured. Remember to create multiple key performance indicators for each strategy to help measure progress.

CONSTRUCT ALL STRATEGIES FOR THE NEW SHORT TERM. The new short term is a time horizon of three years. Strategies that take longer than three years to fully implement should be trimmed so that they fit within a three-year window. If you have strategies that are longer than three years, they should be discarded or redrafted. We are trying to find the sweet spot where your organization will have enough time to implement strategies, but not too much time so that market changes start to impact the efficacy of the strategies. That time horizon, as of now, is about three years.

LEAVE THE LONG-TERM FUZZY, BUT IN VIEW. While creating strategies with a three-year time horizon for implementation, keep an eye toward the longer term. You will want an idea of where this whole thing is headed, but you will have to get comfortable with keeping it fuzzy. Understand that detailing action beyond three years will be expensive and ineffective. Part of the reason for keeping the long term fuzzy is to retain flexibility. Having a death grip on something written down from more than three years ago that clearly won't work in the present is just fear of change making another appearance. Leaving things fuzzy will allow your organization to more easily change directions as conditions warrant.

USE YOUR TEAM. You have feedback and suggestions about how the strategies should look, and so does your team. Your team is an invaluable resource for feedback and suggestions about what strategies best align with the mission of the organization. Work your team into the process early and often. Not only will you receive better ideas, but you will see more genuine buy-in on chosen strategies. Don't worry about the outdated concept that "leadership needs to have it all figured out." These are rapidly changing times that necessitate insight from wherever it can be found. Leaders no longer need to have it all figured out, but they do need to get it figured out.

COMMUNICATE STRATEGIES WIDELY AND OFTEN. Strategies, like the mission, should be understood by every person in the organization, or every person at the team level. If I showed up at your workplace and found a random team member, that team member should be able to summarize the organizational strategies and their team's strategies. Just like with the mission, future leaders should communicate the strategy often.

One effective way of getting it to stick with people is embedding the concepts in stories. Are there any case studies you can use to help illustrate the strategy? Where has there been success that can be made into a story? Stories activate something inside our brains that force us to pay attention.

In addition, share the written strategy. Print a summary of the strategy that can be digested easily. Bring it up at your regular meetings. As the strategy tweaks or changes from time to time, update everyone. Strategy should be alive!

EVALUATE PROGRESS. Are any of the strategies working? How do you know? Implementing strategies is only one part of the process. The other part is evaluating the effectiveness of those strategies.

Evaluation has three parts. The first part is evaluating progress on the key performance indicators. Is the organization, or the team, making progress on the key performance indicators? This is relatively straightforward as the key performance indicators should be clear enough to track progress.

The second part is evaluating the key performance indicators' impact on the strategy. Were the right key performance indicators created in the first place? If there is progress on a key performance indicator, but little progress on the strategy, then there might be something wrong with the key performance indicator. It may need to be refined, or scrapped in favor of a new one.

The third part is evaluating the strategy itself. If the right key performance indicators were selected, and if there is progress being made on those key performance indicators, then the strategy should be coming to life as well. Is the strategy doing what you had hoped?

There is no ego bruise with trying a strategy that doesn't work. In fact, think about strategy in terms of a game. Keep score about what is working and what is not working. Maybe part of a strategy is working, but it needs to be tweaked. The point is to evaluate progress and make quick decisions based on the data.

Share the results of the evaluations often and widely. Keep your team and the organization apprised of progress of any strategy toward fulfilling the mission. Your people are desperately looking to fit their work into a broader context. This is one way to help provide that context.

LET STRATEGY BE DYNAMIC. The old-style creation of strategy meant the organization would set aside a massive amount of time and assemble a committee of people to do the work of creating a strategic plan. The committee would meet and brainstorm and draft ideas. Maybe they would have brought in a consultant to assist. The plan would get longer and more complex as each committee member "added value" to the process. Charts and tables and graphics would be created and added. The plan started talking about initiatives five, seven, or ten years out. Then, finally, after a number of months, the strategic plan was completed and adopted. It would have been printed and bound and distributed.

The people would read the strategic plan, nod their heads, and then place the document on their desk for a few weeks to show others they were invested. Soon, the plan was moved from the desk to the bookshelf. Soon, the plan was moved from an upper shelf on the bookcase to a lower shelf. Soon, the people went back to their email.

Now, this may sound like a really ineffective strategic planning process and rollout, and that's because it is. The point should not be lost. Whatever the lengthy and involved process looked like then will not work today. Instead, keep strategy light and dynamic!

Nobody should be attached to any one strategy, only the outcomes of the strategies. This kind of attitude creates flexibility. Strategy becomes something that organizations and team members work on regularly. It becomes incorporated into the work. It is fluid.

LAST WORD ON STRATEGY

In the Future Leadership Framework, strategy is an essential skill. Strategy is directly related to the future leader's ability to find and respond to the right problems. Being able to create strategies that help the organization advance on its mission will be critical in the years ahead as the forces of generational churn and rapid technological advancement attempt to add new layers of friction. The response to these forces means that strategic plans should become lighter, and will be subject to change more frequently, than in years past, and that these strategic plans will (thankfully) become shorter and clearer.

KEY IDEA

Strategy is about planning the forward actions an organization will take to make progress toward its mission. Strategy requires that the future leader understand where the organization is today, and where it wants to be over the longer term. Strategy also requires that the future leader account for the "winds" that are influencing the organization.

KEY DIFFERENCES

Yesterday's Leader

Fails to link strategy to mission
Fails to create key performance indicators
Rigidly follows the plan

The Future Leader

Always links strategy to mission
Understands and aligns the cascade
Evaluates and makes changes to the plan

KEY QUESTION

If asked, could your team members communicate a clear understanding of the organization's (or team's) strategies and progress on those strategies?

10

INTERACTIVITY

THE FUTURE LEADER'S ABILITY TO ENROLL MEMBERS OF THE FUTURE ORGANIZATION

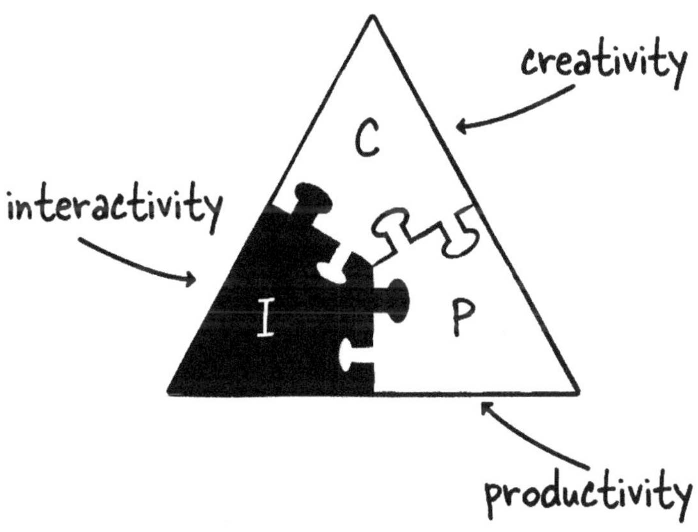

Working with machines requires a very different modus operandi than working with people. Machines have an operating manual and a prescribed method for interaction. Machines, at least for now, are linear. We know that replacing the fried motherboard will bring a broken machine back into full production. Machines don't have "off" days. They don't seek their purpose. They just execute on tasks.

People are different. We are complex. We are emotional. We are creative. Our needs vary greatly. There is no ability to replace a broken motherboard in a person and then achieve instant full capacity. People aren't machines, and the future leader instinctively understands that they can't be treated as such.

In the future, people will continue to be any organization's greatest asset in addition to becoming their greatest point of differentiation. The question is, how should future leaders interact with others to best fulfill the organization's mission?

Interactivity is the second puzzle piece of the Future Leadership Framework and is defined as "acting in such a way as to have an effect on another."[1] Interactivity is the ability of the future leader to enroll others in the future organization. Enrollment, in this sense, happens when people unify around a common mission. This ability is about getting people invested in their work, invested in the organization and its mission, and invested in you as a leader. This is already hard to do, and it may be harder to do in the future.

A future workplace where consistent turnover becomes the norm requires future leaders who can quickly start implementing the skills of Interactivity with their team. To complicate matters, as influence continues to shift from the older generation to the younger generations, future leaders will work amid a new dynamic that may make it more difficult to interact effectively.

The ability to effectively interact is not only subject to generational issues. It is also affected by technological advancement. Many technological innovations seek to digitize the analog leadership ability required to effectively work with people. We have software applications that attempt to help leaders communicate better. We have social media applications that attempt to create connection. We have intranets that seek to answer organizational questions. Despite these advances, interactivity cannot hide behind a technological barrier. It is necessarily an in-person leadership activity.

Mastering the skills that make up the Interactivity ability is what will set you apart as a leader. While others overlook the importance of generational churn and seek to automate more of their leadership, you will take another path and end up way ahead. These skills will not only make you more valuable in the marketplace, but more effective at moving your organization toward its goals despite the challenges.

The next three chapters cover the three most important skills that make up this ability. You will learn how to build relationships that achieve results, how to improve your emotional intelligence to better connect with others, and how to cultivate an environment of trust.

Let's get started.

11

Relationships

DEVELOP THE CURRENCY OF THE FUTURE ORGANIZATION

It's the study that put the term "long" in longitudinal. The Grant Study started in 1938 with 238 Harvard sophomores to better understand the factors that led to a happy and healthy life. Named after W.T. Grant, the owner of the mass-merchandise store, Grant's, the study continues to follow the lives of these Harvard men. Only nineteen members of the original study are still alive, and these men are now in their nineties.[1]

The purpose of the study was relatively straight forward when it started. Arlie Bock, a Harvard physician and founder of the study, wanted to examine what forces produced "normal" young men. Normal he defined as "that combination of sentiments and physiological factors which in total is commonly interpreted as successful living."[2]

While trying to ascertain what factors created normal young men was the reason for the work, the overall goal of the work was something a bit grander. In a 1943 article for *The Harvard Crimson*, Bock noted that "our society has an overabundance of disharmony, frustration, and lack of leadership."[3] He concluded that to alleviate these problems we needed to better understand the secrets of the successful. Once we know how successful men tick, the rest of us could borrow their secrets for our own lives.

Dr. George Vaillant took over as head of the study starting in the 1960s. He interacted with and observed these men for over four decades. In 2008, Vaillant was asked what he had learned from the Grant Study men. His response: the only thing that really matters are your relationships. In fact, he goes on to note that the strongest predictor of life satisfaction is strong relationships.[4] For the man who spent his career studying people to understand what makes them happy, George Vaillant contends that connection is the "whole shooting match."[5]

The only thing that really matters in life are your relationships? Connection is the whole shooting match? These are big statements. And while these conclusions have come from one of the greatest longitudinal studies ever undertaken, the power of relationships is supported elsewhere.

Better Relationships Are Good for Healing

In 2005, researchers from the Department of Psychiatry at The Ohio State University published their findings on how the quality of a marriage can affect the ability to physically heal.

Forty-two healthy married couples aged twenty-two to seventy-seven participated in the study. The average length of time these couples were married was eleven years. The results of this study highlighted a conclusion most of us might intuitively understand to be true. Specifically, those couples who were more hostile toward each other only healed at 60 percent of the rate of couples that were less hostile toward each other.[6] In essence, the quality of your marriage determines the speed at which you physically heal. Relationships matter.

Small Networks Are Not Healthy

It's not only the quality of your relationships that matters, it's also the quantity. A Duke University study has shown that not having enough relationships is also a problem. It turns out that social isolation increases the risks for heart disease patients to suffer further or die from their diseases. Researchers discovered that if a patient had a support network of less than three people, they were more than twice as likely to die as compared to patients with larger support networks.[7] Relationships may be a more powerful force in our lives than we realize.

Relationships Affect Employee Productivity

Gallup has polled more than 15 million employees around the world with this question: "Do you have a best friend at work?" Notice the wording. Gallup asks about a "best" friend because the research has shown that a best friend is a more powerful predictor of workplace outcomes than either a "regular" friend or even a "good" friend.[8]

Do you have a best friend at work? If you do, then you are among the 30 percent of other workers out there. Gallup has found that those who do have a best friend at work are way more likely to be engaged with their work, work better with customers, produce higher quality work, and are less likely to get injured.[9] Having a best friend at work can make you much better at your work.

Since most of us don't have a best friend at work, all can't be lost, right? What about those of us who have regular work friends? Well, it turns out that we might be OK after all.

One Massachusetts Institute of Technology study used tiny sensors to evaluate employee productivity. The MIT researchers used these sensors to track the wearer's movements on a second-by-second basis. These sensors captured motion and audio and transmitted the wearer's position. Researchers could also tell whether the wearer was walking around or, if seated, what their body movements were. The research was seeking to discover which work habits when combined with data on productivity were most effective, and what social networks were most valuable.[10]

The research led to two findings. First, that the more rhythmic the participants were in their work, the more productive they ended up being. The second finding was that when an employee knew many of their colleagues and interacted with them regularly, their productivity increased.[11]

This would seem intuitive if you imagined that the study participant was interacting with her colleagues on work-related matters. After all, people help other people get things done. Counterintuitively, according to the study, the interactions did not have to be work focused. Even the proverbial water cooler conversations were similarly effective at increasing productivity.[12] Our relationships at work, whether we have a best friend or just regular work friends, have a direct correlation to our level of productivity.

THE FUTURE OF RELATIONSHIPS

The art of building and maintaining effective relationships while eliminating harmful relationships is an essential skill in the Future Leadership Framework. Relationships are so important that I have dubbed them the "currency of the future organization." Since all meaningful and significant work requires the help of others at some point, nurturing relationships will continue to be how business best gets done in future organizations.

Think back to the first day on the job you currently have. Remember the compounded discomfort of learning all the basics about the job itself, and not really knowing the people around you. Now, remember those early work relationships where you were trying to get others moving on something you needed. The interactions felt more transactional in nature. Whether you were asking them to review the work and make comments, sign off on the work that was done, or some other request, those interactions came with just a bit of friction. The friction of new people working together.

The interactions likely became easier as time passed. You knew who to approach with different questions. You knew who would take thirty minutes out of their afternoon to help you talk out a problem. You knew somebody who knew somebody else that could help get the project unstuck. Things began to flow just a bit better after your relationships improved.

As the years pass, you end up meeting more people and developing closer relationships. If you have ever held a position for several years, then you have probably experienced how some relationships have become even more enjoyable to you personally, not just professionally. In a large organization where I worked for almost ten years I eventually developed relationships with a number of people who could help me solve whatever type of problem came up. I knew the informal power structure within the organization, and I knew who was more toxic than helpful. In my last few years at the organization, I noticed many of the senior leaders retiring out. Each retirement meant I had to start all over with somebody new. This same dynamic is playing out in a number of organizations and is one component complicating future leaders' ability to master the skill of Relationships.

Relationships and Generational Churn

Generational churn affects relationship-building in a few ways. First, it becomes harder to build great relationships when the relationship participants haven't worked together for very long. The average job tenure right now in all industries and for workers from every generation is only about four years.[13] We saw from a previous chapter that job tenure is positively correlated with age. Older employees tend to stay in jobs in longer, and younger employees tend to switch jobs more often. Baby Boomers have an average tenure of about ten years, but Millennials tend to have a much shorter job tenure.

Time on the job, and time in the organization, are important components of building effective relationships. It takes time to meet new people and it takes a certain amount of time for the serendipity of everyday events to transpire before those relationships move into something more meaningful. And, it also takes time to develop relationships outside the organization that will help you get work done. Vendor relationships, customer relationships, and teaming relationships with other organizations take time.

As longevity in the organization shrinks from retirements and opportunities elsewhere, relationships take a hit. The pace of people cycling through will speed up in the years ahead as Boomers continue to retire out and younger generations move up. While we don't know yet if job tenure will increase as the Millennials get older, we can reasonably assess that the average tenure will decrease in the interim as the workforce skews younger.

There is another generational factor affecting future leaders' ability to cultivate meaningful relationships, and it has to do with generational preferences. We know that the older generation has just recently become outnumbered by the younger generation at work. We also know that different generations have different preferences. As the age gap widens, these preferences can become more pointedly different.

For the Boomer or Millennial, it can be easy to discount the need to build real relationships outside of their age cohort. I have heard plenty of fifty- and sixty-somethings say that they "just need to make it a few more years" before they can escape the madness of trying to integrate with the younger generations. Yes, it's hard to do, and it is also hard for us Gen Xers and Millennials.

Boomers can't ignore half of the office that will be made up of Millennials by the year 2020. This doesn't mean a Boomer needs to adopt a Millennial's way of thinking, or that a Millennial needs to change to become more like a Boomer. It does mean that everyone will need to put in the effort to build relationships across generational divides. The caveat I would add here is this: In any work relationship, it is incumbent on the leader to bend as much as possible. Future leaders don't make others bend to their will, instead they bend as much as possible for the overall health of the organization. After all, future leaders have the ultimate responsibility for the success of the organization.

Relationships and Tech

Generational churn isn't the only factor in all of this. Tech also plays a huge role in complicating the future leader's ability to build and maintain relationships.

It seems we are trying to invent ourselves out of the need to communicate face-to-face. It started with email, grew with smartphones, and is continuing to grow with social media. Many companies use Slack, an online messaging platform, to facilitate organizational discussion. Slack is faster than email at getting thoughts out to the team, but is not a substitute for real relationships, which have always required consistent face time. We have to see each other and be around each other to grow relationships. Nothing can replace the magic that happens when two people sit down and talk.

Still, messaging applications and email are only growing in popularity because they make communicating a message easier. For instance, if the whole team needs to stay a few extra hours to meet a deadline, the fastest way to let everyone know is through an email or a Slack message. These platforms cut down on the time it takes to broadcast a message. It is certainly faster than talking to each person individually.

Another reason we prefer to use tech to communicate is a bit more subtle. When we communicate digitally, there is no ability to gauge reactions in real time. Sending an email telling everyone to stay late won't elicit the immediate and human feedback that you would receive if you were to tell everyone the same news face-to-face. This reduction in friction saves the communicator emotional energy, and saving emotional energy is *very* appealing.

If you have ever asked somebody to do something at work that they didn't want to do, then you know what I am talking about. Asymmetrical communication, like email, removes the emotional expenditure that is natural in micro-confrontations. You probably won't get a terse email in response to your request to stay late. You probably won't get any feedback at all unless someone has a commitment and they can't stay. Technology has made it so much easier to break bad news! Though we might save the momentary emotional expenditure, we are simultaneously losing the other benefits of real relationships.

The future leader needs to understand this. The allure of technology is that it becomes much easier to fire off an email than it is to walk over and check in. Face-to-face time should not be the only way leaders communicate, but leaders should be intentional about its use. If building and maintaining relationships is important, and if we have a shorter window in which to build relationships because of turnover, and if we have technology that is tempting us as an alternative to face-to-face time, then the future leaders need to be prepared to respond.

BUILDING EFFECTIVE RELATIONSHIPS

Here are a few ideas for future leaders when it comes to building and maintaining relationships.

THE VALUE OF ANY RELATIONSHIP IS THE RELATIONSHIP ITSELF. The internet and the speed of business has tarnished the way some of us view relationships. Relationships, both inside and outside of work, should never be only transactional. Meaning, future leaders should see making and building connections with other people as the end goal. Seeing it this way will help you start building new relationships more quickly, which will be necessary in the future workplace as the speed of turnover increases.

UNDERSTAND THAT RELATIONSHIPS BUILD TRUST. We tend to trust the people we have a relationship with more than others we are only loosely connected to. We saw earlier that a third of us don't trust the organizations we work for. One way to narrow this trust gap is by quickly building and maintaining real relationships. When others in the workplace see that we are invested in them as people and that we genuinely care about them, we can gain their trust.

UNDERSTAND THAT RELATIONSHIPS BUILD BETTER TEAMS. A team is a composition of people working on a common objective. Building better relationships will help the team be more successful by promoting team cohesion. In addition, by creating a number of relationships inside and outside the organization, the future leader also identifies potential people who could be a good fit for the team.

CONTINUALLY BUILD AND STRENGTHEN YOUR RELATIONSHIPS. Each relationship requires some level of nurturing to build into its full potential. I have a good friend that I have known for over thirty years. We grew up one door apart. I don't hold this relationship in the same way I hold my other relationships. It's different. And though I treat it differently than other relationships in some respects, I try to take the time to build and strengthen each relationship I have—albeit imperfectly. In the workplace, this concept might mean having more than occasional lunches with other employees, (happily) attending or organizing workplace events, or contributing to organizational committees. Engaging in bits of small talk as the opportunities arise can also help.

ALL GREAT RELATIONSHIPS ARE BUILT OVER TIME. There are no shortcuts here. We need to start building work relationships much faster because we can assume the other party will move on quickly.

In my last job, I intentionally built cross-department relationships over several years. It was a continuous process of checking in, making small talk, helping on projects, attending meetings, going to lunch, and more. There is no work of substance you can successfully bring to market without relationships. You might be able to do the technical part of the work in solitude, but any project will always depend on getting other people on board at some time and in some way. Look at the long arc when it comes to relationships and consider new relationships to be a long-term investment. Building relationships for the long term also means keeping in touch with certain people who have moved on. Just because you no longer work together doesn't mean the relationship needs to end. I wouldn't encourage you to maintain every relationship, but I would encourage you to maintain the ones that stood out to you.

HELP OTHERS BUILD RELATIONSHIPS. We want to make our organizations as sticky as possible so that great people stay. Part of encouraging people to stay is making sure they feel connected to the organization and to their team. Without this connection, it becomes too easy to leave for a $5,000-per-year pay raise. As a future leader, help to facilitate those connections. This may mean you host lunches with your team or with other teams in the organization. It may mean putting together happy hours for people to mingle. It may mean creating an intranet program that automatically introduces users to other people in the organization. Whatever the action is, your goal should be to help facilitate the creation of relationships among others.

While you are doing this, remember that the connections you help facilitate do not need to be solely strategic. As mentioned earlier, the connection is where the value is, whatever else arises out of that connection should be considered a bonus.

DON'T BE AFRAID TO GET PERSONAL. Business is not business anymore. All business is becoming more personal and that is not a bad thing. The younger generations expect to have different relationships in the organization than the older generations had. The leaders who are all business are missing out on the opportunity to build relationships that help team members stick around.

Go ahead. Ask about their weekends. Go a few questions deep on that movie they just watched. No need to go over the top on this, but take a minute each day to connect with your people on a deeper level. It lets them know that you care about them.

TREAT YOUR TEAM MEMBERS AS PEOPLE FIRST. Your team members should be treated as people first, and employees second. We are not automatons. We are people who have family and friends and lives outside of our careers. For the leaders who can see their team members as people first, it will help positively color the relationship while at work.

SAY "THANK YOU" OFTEN. Make sure to thank your team for their efforts on a regular basis. This shouldn't be shouting "thank you!" from inside your cubicle as they brush past you heading home. Each thank you should be personalized to the person and to the work that you are recognizing them for. That's where its power comes from. If you have a team member who has really stepped up on a project, then take the time to notice their efforts. If you have a team member who has taken on extra work after someone else quit, let them know that you appreciate it. When we say, "thank you," we are taking time to recognize the other person. We are letting them know that we see them and we see the effort they have put in. Do this in a sincere way, and do it more often than you think you should.

DON'T SHY AWAY FROM ENDING RELATIONSHIPS THAT NEED TO END. Just because you have a relationship on some level with somebody doesn't necessarily mean that relationship needs to continue on indefinitely. Some relationships are more of a fit than others. Some naturally lend themselves to a long-term arrangement. Many others don't. As a future leader, ending relationships may mean you need to move people off the team, or move people out the door. You may need to move contracted help off the project. Be prepared for that. As great as the right relationships can be, there is nothing more toxic than a bad relationship. Be brave and end relationships that need to end.

LAST WORD ON RELATIONSHIPS

Building and maintaining relationships is a critical skill in the Future Leadership Framework. What makes this skill difficult for most people is getting the relationship started. Meeting new people and taking the time to bring them into your world is emotionally taxing. It's much easier to friend someone on Facebook.

Technology will make it easier to connect with people digitally, but technology will never be able to help you build the real relationships that good work always requires. Adding to the appeal of technology that attempts to create and manage relationships for you is the force of generational churn. Turnover is speeding up in organizations of all sizes. The combination of these forces means that future leaders will have to leave their individual workspaces more now than in years past.

KEY IDEA

Building and maintaining relationships can make you and your team healthier, happier, and more productive. This ancient human skill is being undermined by the forces of generational churn and rapid technological advancement. The future leader who focuses on building relationships despite these potentially eroding forces will be more effective at executing on the mission of the organization.

KEY DIFFERENCES

Yesterday's Leader

Keeps relationships transactional
Is slow to start new relationships
Relies too much on technology

The Future Leader

Understands relationships' intrinsic value
Quickly starts new relationships
Uses technology appropriately

KEY QUESTION

How well do you know your team members outside of their professional role?

12

Empathy

USE EMOTIONAL INTELLIGENCE TO MOVE OTHERS

PHINEAS GAGE LIVED. This doesn't seem like a profound statement, except that in a workplace accident on September 13, 1848, Gage had a straight iron bar that was forty-three inches long and weighed more than thirteen pounds, rocket through his head.

Gage, then twenty-five, was the foreman of a crew cutting a railroad bed in Cavendish, Vermont, for the Rutland and Burlington Railroad. Black rock was getting in the way of the future rail line, and the best way to remove rock like this was blasting.

Rock blasting back then, like rock blasting today, starts in a similar way. Workers drill holes into rock to place the explosives. This is where the similarities end. Back then, after drilling holes, loose powder would be placed and tamped into the hole with a straight iron bar. The powder they used was explosive, so the work had to be done carefully. Sparks would have had consequences.

After placing loose powder in the hole, workers would fill the remainder of the hole with sand. The nonexplosive sand was tamped down aggressively to create a tight pack of material in the hole. Once everything is packed in, the crew would move away before detonating the powder. The explosion would split the rock.

On that September day in 1848, Gage made a mistake while

setting the blasting powder. He aggressively tamped the powder in the hole with his iron bar as if it were sand. A spark ignited the powder. The explosion turned the iron bar he was using into a missile that shot up and out of the hole in the rock.

The skyward launch of the tamping bar would have been a cool sight, except that Gage's head was in the way. The speed and power of the bar traveling upward tore a hole from his left eye through the top of his head. The bar was found several feet away "smeared with blood and brain." Amazingly, Gage lived.

This story, as I first heard it from Dr. Travis Bradberry in a keynote, had me on the edge of my seat. Bradberry is a psychologist and coauthor of the book *Emotional Intelligence 2.0*. He went on to describe what happened to Gage after the accident.

The projectile had essentially removed the front left side of Gage's brain. This part of the brain is known as the prefrontal cortex, or PFC. The PFC is responsible for our executive functions. The *Indian Journal of Psychiatry* notes that the PFC integrates various sensory modalities "...in a precise fashion to form the physiologic constructs of memory, perception, and diverse cognitive processes."[2] In other words, this is an important part of the brain when it comes to expression of our emotions, judgment, impulse control, and decision-making, among other functions. As a result of losing part of his PFC, Gage turned into a different person.

John Harlow was the physician who treated Gage after the accident and noted later in a professional journal that "his [Gage's] contractors, who regarded him as the most efficient and capable foreman in their employ previous to his injury, considered the change in his mind so marked that they could not give him his place again."[2] Harlow went on to note that Gage was "...fitful, irreverent, indulging at times in the grossest profanity (which was not previously his custom), manifesting but little deference for his fellows, impatient of restraint of advice when it conflicts with his desires, at times pertinaciously obstinate [sic]..."[3] The accident irrevocably changed how Gage expressed himself, which changed how others perceived him.

No doubt this is a fascinating case study on the lingering effects of a traumatic brain injury, but what does it have to do with the skill of Empathy for future leaders? This case study illustrates the importance of emotional intelligence. Gage, like the rest of us, had the gift of experiencing emotion, but, unlike the rest of us, had little ability to manage the expression of those emotions after the accident. The fallout affected Gage until his early death.

The vast majority of us acquire some level of emotional intelligence as we grow up. Early in our lives we learn how to interact with our friends, our parents, and our acquaintances. At some point for many of us, though, we get to a certain level of emotional intelligence and then we stop learning. The good news is that we can become even more emotionally intelligent. And, becoming more emotionally intelligent is a skill that will be critical for the future leader.

EMOTIONAL INTELLIGENCE FOR FUTURE LEADERS

Emotion has been defined as "a conscious mental reaction (such as anger or fear) subjectively experienced as strong feeling usually directed toward a specific object and typically accompanied by physiological and behavioral changes in the body."[4] Emotional intelligence is your ability to recognize emotions in yourself and others, and the ability to use this information to better manage your behavior and relationships.

From Bradberry's work on the subject, emotional intelligence is the sum of two competencies: personal competency and social competency. Each of these competencies is composed of two skills.[5]

The **personal competency** part of emotional intelligence is made up of **self-awareness** and **self-management**. The **self-awareness** skill is being able to accurately identify what emotion you are experiencing, and the **self-management** skill is being able to control your response to an emotion.

The **social competency** part of emotional intelligence is made up of **social awareness** and **relationship management**. The **social awareness** skill is accurately identifying emotions as they are happening to someone you are interacting with, while the **relationship management** skill is your ability to manage relationships you have with others to a beneficial outcome.

Do you see a link between the competencies? Each requires you to make an assessment about what emotion is at play and to create behavior that leads to beneficial outcomes. We have no ability to control whether we experience an emotion, but we do have the ability to recognize, label, and control our responses to our emotions.

Why Control Behavior in the First Place?

In talking about what emotional intelligence is, we blew past a fundamental question: Why should the behavior that follows emotion be controlled in the first place? Why should a leader pause and not vent explosive comments when bad news breaks? Why should a leader constrain their erratic happy dance after receiving great news?

The answer is because deploying the skill of emotional intelligence is effective in the workplace. The *Industrial Psychiatry Journal* notes that "the role of EI [emotional intelligence] in achieving organizational effectiveness is very significant, and it is reiterated in studies carried out across the globe."[6] Daniel Goleman in his 2002 book, *Primal Leadership* notes that, "...the higher the rank of those considered star performers, the more EI competencies emerged as the reason for their effectiveness."[7] The reason you should care about this is because emotional intelligence can help you be a better leader.

Emotional Intelligence and Generational Churn

One of the core tenets of emotional intelligence is empathy. Empathy is the ability to recognize and understand the feelings others are having. For the future leader contending with the fallout from massive generational change, being empathetic is important.

The workplace is fundamentally changing and Boomers role in the workplace is also fundamentally changing. Because of this, Boomers are undergoing an identity shift of sorts. If you think there aren't any deep feelings around this, you would be mistaken. Frustration, anger, irritation, elation, and all emotions in between are likely seeping out of the Boomers and into the workplace on a regular basis as a result.

The future leader should be on the lookout for emotions that come bubbling up to the surface about this identity change. "Those young people have no idea what's going on!" "This isn't the way we used to do it." "I guess we'll just see what happens." What you are hearing are expressions of emotion. These expressions may be directed at others in the organization, but they really say more about the person doing the expressing. The question, coming back to emotional intelligence, is what can future leaders do to identify those emotions, and how can future leaders work productively and respectfully considering those emotions?

Identity isn't only a Boomer issue. A similar kind of identity change is happening on the other end of the spectrum with the

Millennials. As their representation in the workplace surges in the years ahead, so too will their influence. But just because they have the influence doesn't mean they will have it all figured out. Power that lacks experience and, hence, wisdom, is fraught. The Millennials are also experiencing a shift in their identity away from the free spirit of youth and into the sober (and more boring) realm of personal responsibility and accountability. The next several years will be hard for them as it will be hard for the Boomers. Future leaders will need to be tuned to expressions of emotion, and what those emotions mean, for each of the generations in the workplace.

Emotional Intelligence Supercharges the Future Leadership Framework Skills

Keep in mind that this is a time of massive change and it won't be easy for future leaders either. We need more emotionally intelligent leaders now than ever before. As you make investments in this skill, the dividends will work to supercharge the other Future Leadership Framework skills.

In fact, the real horsepower comes when this skill is used in conjunction with the other skills in the framework. For instance, part of building and implementing a proper mission is fostering stakeholder buy-in. The emotionally intelligent future leader attempting to create or revise an organizational or a team mission will have a better chance at creating this buy-in.

Or, take the skill of Trust coming up in the next chapter. The emotionally intelligent leader will be able to create an environment of trust much easier than an emotionally unintelligent one. In this way, the power of emotional intelligence is not only in the skill itself, but in how the skill amplifies the effectiveness of the other skills.

DEVELOPING BETTER EMOTIONAL INTELLIGENCE

When it comes to emotional intelligence, you can't go from zero to fully competent by reading a single chapter in a book, but you can use the following ideas to get started.

LEARN MORE ABOUT EMOTIONAL INTELLIGENCE. The book *Emotional Intelligence 2.0* by Travis Bradberry and Jean Greaves is a great place to start. This book can be read in a few hours and comes with an offer to take an online test to measure your emotional intelligence. Also, if you do an online search for "emotional intelligence" and "HBR" (for *Harvard Business Review*) there are a number of great articles that go deeper into the topic. Do the reading.

EMOTIONS ARE PART OF THE PACKAGE. If you have been entrusted with leading people, then understand that emotions are part of the package. Emotions are not a flaw, they are simply a part of being human. You may interact with people who cry at work. You may interact with hot-tempered people. You may interact with people who automatically squelch their feelings because they believe emotions are not appropriate for the workplace. Leadership is about working well with people, and people are emotional beings. The sooner we understand that emotions are part of the package, the sooner we can move on to effective ways of handling emotion in ourselves and others.

WORK TO CONSCIOUSLY IDENTIFY THE EMOTION. While there are only five categories of core emotions, there are many different words to describe the variation of any particular core emotion.

For instance, happiness is a core emotion. But maybe in the moment you don't necessarily feel happy, you feel contented. Maybe you are experiencing joy or excitement. All of these fall into the same bucket labeled "happiness." Consciously identifying the emotion means figuring out the right word for the variation of the core emotion, and then figuring out which core emotion that variation falls under.

Start by actively identifying the emotion. "The emotion I am feeling right now is ______." I know you might be thinking that this seems easy, but have you ever consciously done this? I didn't until a few years ago. And most of the time, I still don't. But when you put conscious effort into it, identifying the core emotion can make the feelings, and the potential response to those feelings, much clearer. In addition, I have found that labeling a negative emotion helps control my response to that emotion. It eliminates some of the emotion's power.

CONSCIOUSLY SEEK TO UNDERSTAND YOUR EXPRESSION OF AN EMOTION. Now that you have figured out what the emotion is, you are poised to better respond to that emotion. If you can manage to insert just a sliver of daylight between the stimulus and your immediate emotional response, not only can you identify the core emotion, but you can better control the response to that emotion. It is easy to think that our responses are simply our responses and that's the way it is. But emotional intelligence is about changing this narrative, controlling our reactions, and continuing to move in a beneficial direction.

Venting anger because somebody said they would have the report to you by five p.m. and now it's going to be late won't actually solve the problem, though it may help you feel better in the moment. Venting may, however, alienate you from the person who is delivering the bad news and potentially create an ongoing rift. I have found that the personal relief of a knee-jerk response to an emotional trigger is often short-lived, but fallout from a bad response lasts way longer than I want it to.

DETERMINE HOW YOU WOULD RATHER RESPOND. What would the right response look like? To help answer this question, consider the following two steps. First, determine which of the five emotions really gets under your skin. Which is your favorite flavor? Mine is the "afraid" emotion. Being fearful really bothers me, and as I get older, I have found it easier than it should be to fall down the rabbit hole of fear over things that really shouldn't provoke such a response.

Understanding which of the five emotions hits you hardest is an essential first step. The second step is to visualize how you would prefer to respond to the emotion that bugs you the most. How will you act in the presence of this emotion? This is essentially practicing for the emotional response before the emotion arises. Practicing for the emotional response can help increase your comfort when the next trigger for that emotion presents itself. This is not only effective for your "favorite" emotion, but it is also an effective practice for other emotions as well.

SEEK TO OBSERVE AND IDENTIFY EMOTIONS IN OTHERS. This requires the future leader to have enough situational awareness to shift away from only participating in the interaction to observing the interaction from a detached perspective. What emotions do you hear from your team members? What words are they using? What body postures do you see? People offer up a staggering number of clues about how they are really feeling. It is up to the future leader to see these clues, interpret them, and then take action.

ASSIGN MEANING SLOWLY. Like seeing patterns, another component of our human operating system is that we quickly assign meaning to other people's actions. Have you ever created a story about someone's actions that put them in the worst possible light only to find out later that there was some fact you missed? If you remember nothing else from this chapter, remember this: assign meaning slowly. More often than not you will pick up information in fragments over time. You hear one side of the story today, and the other side of the story tomorrow. You receive a brusque email today, and then a follow-up email that apologizes. Someone is late on a project and you hear later that they were dealing with a death in the family. Hold off on making judgments until you have more information. This is also good training for delaying the knee-jerk response to a stimulus.

LAST WORD ON EMOTIONAL INTELLIGENCE

I took my first emotional-intelligence evaluation in October 2015 through TalentSmart. In October 2017, I completed an updated assessment. My scores in both the personal and social competencies improved because I had spent time working on the skills, but it was clear that I had more work to do.

The reason I spent time on this was because of what I noticed about the leaders who really resonated with me over the years. They all seemed to have a quality I couldn't quite put my finger on. Eventually I figured it out. These leaders not only had the ability to control their own expressions of emotion, but they also read into my emotional architecture. When a land mine of a problem blew up on me at work a few years ago, I had a leader who took a whole day out of his busy work schedule to travel with me from Seattle to Portland, Oregon, to help me clean up the mess I had made. This particular land mine exploded in slow motion over a few weeks—like the elevator shaft explosion scene from *The Matrix*—and managed to spike my favorite "afraid" emotion. Even though his role in helping to clean up my mess was limited, his willingness to make the trip, sit in the meetings, and provide backup showed me that he cared and that I wasn't alone.

KEY IDEA

None of us can control whether we have an emotion, but we can always control how we respond to that emotion. Emotional intelligence is the ability to identify and manage the responses to your own emotions, and the ability to identify emotions in others to help better manage the relationship. Future leaders looking to maximize their effectiveness in the workplace will work on expressing their emotions in a way that promotes beneficial outcomes. Those leaders will also need to notice and work with the emotional reactions of others to maintain good relationships.

KEY DIFFERENCES

Yesterday's Leader

Thinks emotions are inappropriate at work
Assumes their expression of emotion is fixed
Is blind to emotion in others

The Future Leader

Understands emotions are natural
Improves their expression of emotion
Observes and identifies emotions in others

KEY QUESTION

Do you consistently moderate your expressions of emotion at work?

13

Trust

BE RADICALLY TRANSPARENT

WITH A SINGLE MEMO in the winter of 2013, the ability to remotely work for Yahoo! was formally eliminated. Part of the memo read: "To become the absolute best place to work, communication and collaboration will be important, so we need to be working side-by-side. That is why it is critical that we are all present in our offices."[1] The new edict gave Yahoo's remote workers about six months to relocate from wherever they were working back into Yahoo! offices. The new policy was controversial among employees and observers.

I remember hearing about this policy at the time of its release. My initial thought was that the move seemed distinctly out of place. Yahoo!, now owned by Verizon and a part of Oath, is a big search company in the heart of California's Silicon Valley. The general ethos of Silicon Valley is about creating the leading edge of innovation—not just technological innovation, but also innovation in how companies do things. It's a place that makes possible what hasn't been possible before.

This is the place that is trailblazing employee experience. Companies here offer meaningful maternity leave and free gourmet food all day long. Companies here have nap pods and offer unlimited vacation days. And, Silicon Valley is also where IBM pioneered the concept of remote work.

According to its former CEO, Marissa Mayer, Yahoo! managed to become one of only three companies to reach a billion monthly users with a market cap of $43 billion.[2] This was a big-deal company in a big-deal part of the country. Why would a big-deal company like Yahoo! seemingly take a step backward with respect to remote work?

The other thought that popped into my mind as I read about Yahoo's decision was an actual sentence that I heard a few years ago when I was called on the carpet for bending the rules at my organization. I will never forget it. "If you aren't here, then how do we know you are actually working?" (*shudder*) Just thinking about the whole interaction gets me boiling.

A superhero of an engineer who was a part of our small team had a killer commute to the office. Seattle traffic can make you beg for mercy. I knew the commute was getting to him, and I also knew that I didn't want to lose him. The organization wouldn't have approved but we worked out a plan, outside of the official bureaucracy, that allowed him to work from home a day or two per week. In our particular situation, the ability to work remotely was not as easy as it might have been for a Yahoo! employee. Our particular work required us to be on-site for a majority of the time, but we made it work. I knew at some point I would be beaten for taking the initiative, but keeping the engineer was worth it.

THE CURRENT STATE OF TRUST

As I reflect on both situations, the common theme is what was inferred. Both situations seem to infer that the very people who made the organization work cannot be trusted. After all, if you aren't here, how do we know you are actually working?

Richard Branson, the billionaire founder of the Virgin companies, remarked on the trust aspect of Yahoo's decision in a blog post. He said "to successfully work with other people, you have to trust each other. A big part of this is trusting people to get their work done wherever they are, without supervision."[3] At least in Yahoo's situation, the issue of trust was only insinuated. In my situation, trust was at the center of my reprimand. Working remotely requires a degree of trust between the organization and the team member. And trust is tricky.

Trust feels like a classic "I'll know it when I see it" thing. There is no good hard definition I have found that can span all individual experience. The definition I most align with, I found in Brené Brown's book, *Braving the Wilderness*. She quotes from author Charles Feltman, who says that trust is "choosing to risk making something you value vulnerable to another person's actions."[4]

Trusting others means letting them through the walls we have carefully constructed to protect us. Who knows what they will do once they are on the inside!

One misstep is all it takes for us to push the offender back outside the gates. Broken trust is too painful to go unpunished. Trust can take forever to establish, but an instant to destroy. And trust for many organizations and institutions right now is a real problem.

Trust Is Trending Down

The consulting company Edelman recently released its 2017 Edelman Trust Barometer. Their research indicates that we are in "all-time low" for CEO credibility. Only 37 percent of respondents considered CEOs to be credible. Only 29 percent considered government officials to be credible. All twenty-eight countries covered in Edelman's research showed declines in CEO credibility ratings.[5]

Gallup recently reported that confidence in a number of our institutions is low. In one Gallup report, 41 percent of respondents indicated they had a "great deal" or "quite a lot" of confidence in churches. Big business only had 21 percent of respondents with a similar level of confidence. Congress took the lowest ranking with only 12 percent.[6]

Polling from America's most recent presidential election showed that both candidates had big-time problems when ranked for honesty and trustworthiness. Their trust numbers were well below 40 percent.[7]

The American Psychological Association's (APA) 2017 Work and Well Being Survey found that one in five American workers don't trust their employers.[8] In their 2014 survey, the APA noted that a third of respondents didn't believe their employer was always honest and truthful with them.[9]

The data show that trust is an issue for many of us, and the fallout from a lack of trust shows up in our work. One way a lack of trust manifests is through decreased employee engagement.

Trust Affects Employee Engagement

Employee engagement is referring to those people at work who are emotionally and mentally invested in their work and their employer. Engaged employees are not necessarily just the people who are returning emails on the weekend. The engaged aren't necessarily in your face about it, but they are the people who are invested in the work they do and the organization they work for. And, it turns out that engaged workers are really good for organizations.

In a meta-analysis that looked at 263 research studies across 192 organizations in 49 industries and 34 countries, the data show a positive correlation between employee engagement and higher customer ratings, higher profitability, more productivity, lower turnover, lower number of safety incidents, and less absenteeism, among other findings.[10]

Having engaged employees is good for the business because it is profitable. DDI, a leadership consultancy, estimates that moving from low engagement to high engagement in a 10,000-person organization would result in a $42 million improvement.[11]

Willis Towers Watson notes that the average operating margin is three times higher for organizations with high levels of employee engagement as opposed to low levels of engagement.[12] In this same article, Willis Towers Watson notes that engaged employees tend to take about half the time off that disengaged employees take per year.[13] Engaged employees improve productivity and profitability for their organizations.

Another way engagement benefits the organization is by reducing turnover. Turnover, depending on the position the person held, can be expensive. The Center for American Progress notes that the cost of turnover is about 21 percent of one year's salary.[14] So, if the worker was making $50,000 per year, the cost to replace that worker would be about $10,500.

The Society for Human Resource Management notes that it takes an average of forty-two days to fill a job.[15] If we combine these together, then the organization is looking at over a month with a job vacancy and a 20 percent premium to fill one position. And, we can assume this cost is higher in 2018 as organizations struggle to find skilled talent in an employee's job market. The Bureau of Labor Statistics reported that more than 5 million people separated from their jobs in September 2017 alone.[16] Even the best leadership can't stop all great employees from turning over, but slowing the rate of turnover is possible.

Trust can radically decrease turnover. Research has shown that turnover can be reduced by 25 percent in turnover-prone organizations (think retail and fast food), and by 65 percent in low-turnover organizations (think professional positions) with a change in employee engagement.[17]

Trust is the soil that helps grow true employee engagement. One researcher found that high-trust organizations have a workforce that is 76 percent more engaged than low-trust organizations.[18] Conversely, one of the primary reasons for disengagement among employees is a scarcity of trust. Building and maintaining trust in the future organization is a critical skill for future leaders.

TRUST FOR FUTURE LEADERS

Building trust quickly and maintaining a high level of trust will be fundamental for the success of future organizations. New relationships at work may start with a degree of trust, but it is up to the future leaders to build on that by promoting a culture of trust. New people don't know you like the people you have been working with for years. Each new person has a lot on the line when starting a new job in a new organization. Their livelihood is at stake. Ensuring that the organization has a culture of trust starts with the future leader establishing and maintaining that standard. Couple the changing workforce with the ability of technology to amplify any transgression, and authentic trust becomes a necessity.

Amplification of transgressions seems to be what technology does best if you watch the news. With the rise of technology, there is no place to hide anymore. Just recently, a cyclist, on her own time, was photographed flipping off the president's motorcade.[19] The photo went viral and she ended up losing her job. It is possible she would still be employed if this happened just a few years earlier because photographs were harder to take and even harder to disseminate. Now, technology is becoming stunningly great at making visible what was once invisible.

The implication is that acts that establish trust must be authentic, because acts that destroy trust often quickly find a spotlight and an audience. If you consider that building trust is like a slow climb up a snowy hill, ruining trust is like a sled ride to the bottom. It happens fast.

IMPROVING TRUST

The following are some ideas for improving trust in your organization:

CREATE PERSONAL CONNECTION. Nothing will ruin employee engagement and trust more than a disconnected employee. Being disconnected means the employee has few bonds with others in the organization, and there is little personal investment in the organization. The disconnected are showing up most days, but their work is mechanical and uninspired. They aren't having lunch too often with others. They might be overly quiet or they may seem aloof.

Personal connections are built when future leaders expend more emotional effort into relationships. Since the buck stops with the future leader for the overall performance of the organization, the buck also stops with the future leader for helping employees create personal connections. Obviously, you can't make the horse drink, but you can put the bucket of water close by. This may take the form of more team lunches, more daily interaction, or assignment of these employees into other teams (think safety teams, or holiday committees, or other specialized organization teams) where connections can be made.

Building connection in the workplace is an ongoing effort. This is difficult for working leaders. We are all busy. Leadership, though, has the distinct duty of making the teams function as best they are able. Part of this effort is helping team members build connections among each other and with the organization itself.

CONSISTENTLY ALIGN WORDS WITH ACTIONS. In one study involving 386 employees in the top 1,000 manufacturing companies and the top 500 service companies in Taiwan, researchers found that consistency between words and actions is positively related to employee trust.[20] Do we need a study to tell us this? People will listen to what you say, but they watch what you do even more closely. This requires the future leader to become conscious of not only what they say, but what they do. Don't make promises you aren't willing to back up. Big or small, when the two are unaligned, people will notice and assign negative meaning to it.

BE MORE TRANSPARENT THAN YOU THINK YOU NEED TO BE. Technology is not bashful about helping future leaders become more transparent. I often tell my young kids that nothing can be effectively hidden anymore. Everyone has a camera and the ability to shoot 4K video. Social media has made it possible to share any information with an audience. It seems companies and institutions are getting hacked on a daily basis. Like it or not, transparency is being forced upon us. In one sense, this isn't necessarily a bad thing. Future leaders should embrace the concept of being more transparent.

Consider the Colorado company, Namasté Solar. Namasté has posted the salary information for each of its employees for all to see.[21] Imagine knowing the salaries of each of your coworkers. Does that concept make you uncomfortable? This level of transparency may not be right for you, but the larger trend line is bending toward more transparency.

While we are at it, why not embrace the concept of radical transparency? Radical transparency, in this sense, is not saying everything that is on your mind. Rather, this is the kind of transparency that is radical for you. It means being way more open than you may be comfortable being. It doesn't mean being a jerk, but it might mean sharing more than you historically have. Your people can take it. They are adults.

If you bend toward transparency, then it becomes acceptable to share that the organization has hit a rough patch before you have a definitive course of action settled. It means you become much more comfortable saying "I don't know" than you used to be. The more you can share, the better off you will be. People can sense when there are secrets, and it makes them uncomfortable. To make matters worse, when the "secret" finally comes out, it usually isn't that good. The sentiment then turns to "That's it? You couldn't trust me with that?" The secret has done more harm than good. Transparency, on the other hand, promotes a culture of trust.

COMMUNICATE MORE THAN YOU THINK YOU NEED TO. This one I had to learn the hard way. Several years ago I learned that I was not communicating enough with my team. It turns out that since my team wasn't getting the information they needed from me, they were making up their own stories to fill in the gaps in their knowledge. When I later learned about those stories, I cringed. First, the stories were unbelievably wrong. Second, I learned that what I considered to be unimportant information still needed to be shared and shared regularly. Communicate more than you think you need to and it will help you build and maintain a culture of trust.

EMPATHY IS KING. We instinctively trust people who are interested in us, and we instinctively distrust people who are uninterested in us. Using empathy helps communicate that we are interested in our team members. Empathy is the ability to notice and understand the feelings of others. This presupposes that we are listening to our people, and that we care enough to try and see things from their perspective. No longer is business just business. That sentiment is over. Business is now personal. And we need to show up to work as people.

SAY "I DON'T KNOW" MORE OFTEN. We don't verbalize this phrase enough. There is still some subtle old-school stigma attached to admitting that we don't know something. It's time to move past this stigma once and for all. Saying "I don't know" nowadays is a power move. It conveys to people that you are authentic. It also conveys that there is something to figure out. Leaders don't need to have all the answers, but they do need to be willing to figure out the answers.

BE BRAVE WITH BAD NEWS. Creating a culture of trust means future leaders are willing to dish out both the good news and the bad news. For a number of leaders, doling out bad news can feel too emotionally taxing. Instead, they shy away from it, or they minimize it. Leadership is an emotionally taxing role and just because something might feel uncomfortable doesn't mean it's not the right thing to do. Be brave with bad news. By doing so, you will help to maintain a culture of trust.

BE DIRECT AND KIND. Trust happens, in part, when we have a clear read on the other person. To this end, as future leaders, we need to be direct and kind when communicating with others. This means expressing our thoughts clearly, and in a way that leans toward kindness. Just because the news might be bad, doesn't mean it has to be delivered in a negative way.

LAST WORD ON TRUST

Trust is choosing to risk making something you value vulnerable to another person's actions. This will be our working definition of trust. Put yourself in the shoes of those you interact with at work. How much do they trust you? How much do they trust the organization? To be trustworthy, we are in effect saying, "You can give me what you value. I won't ruin it."

Trust, like the other skills in the Future Leadership Framework, can be improved. You aren't born with a certain amount of trust or a certain ability to trust. There is a choice between working to create a culture of trust, and working to create an environment where trust is difficult. If you choose to create a strong culture of trust, then you choose success for your organization. Trust has been shown to increase productivity, increase engagement, increase the bottom line, and, hence, increase your organization's ability to execute on its mission. The verdict is clear.

KEY IDEA

Intentionally promoting a culture of trust will lead to better employee engagement, less turnover, and more productivity. These improvements will have a dramatic impact on the organization's financial performance and the organization's ability to execute on its mission.

KEY DIFFERENCES

Yesterday's Leader

Doesn't think about the importance of trust
Holds on to information
Doesn't align words with action

The Future Leader

Understands the importance of trust
Shares information
Intentionally aligns words and actions

KEY QUESTION

If I asked your employees to rate the level of trust they have in you and in the organization on a scale of 1-10, how would they answer?

14

PRODUCTIVITY

THE FUTURE LEADER'S ABILITY TO GENERATE RESULTS IN THE FUTURE ORGANIZATION

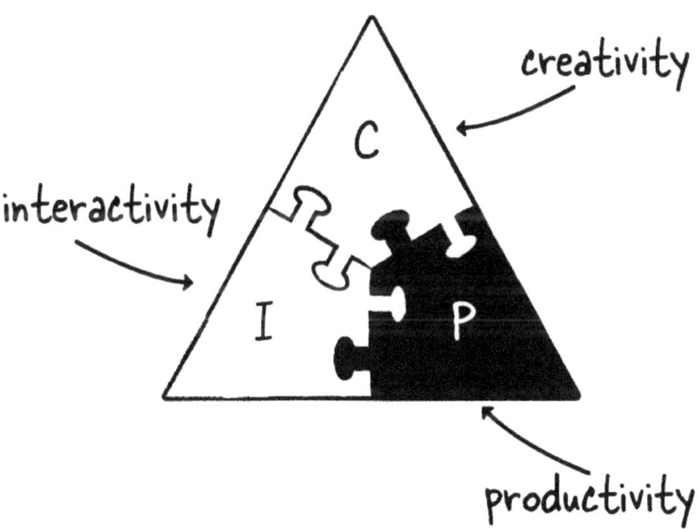

FOR FUTURE LEADERS, the **Creativity** ability is about finding and responding to the right problems in the first place, and the **Interactivity** ability is about enrolling members of the future organization. There is a third piece to the Future Leadership

Framework that, once snapped into place, completes the puzzle. The third puzzle piece is the **Productivity** ability.

As with Creativity, Productivity is different in a leadership context. Most of the leaders I have come across are working leaders, meaning they are also responsible for hands-on, technical work of some kind. To be clear, this ability isn't about improving future leaders' productivity when it comes to the technical part of their work. Rather, it's about creating an environment that helps optimize their team's productivity. The question is: how can future leaders create an environment in which high productivity becomes an unremarkable norm?

Many organizations are already experiencing problems with productivity as the result of underperforming leadership practices. As we have already seen, underperforming leadership is being exacerbated by the forces of generational churn and rapid technological advancement.

Mastering the skills that make up the Productivity ability means you will spend your time, energy, and attention creating a high-performance organization. Over the next four chapters you will learn the "how" and "why" of setting clear expectations that drive results, building effective teams of the future, growing your greatest asset through innovative training, and mastering your own personal organization to keep up-to-speed on all aspects of the work.

Let's get started.

15

Expectations

PROVIDE ABUNDANT CLARITY

THE PITTSBURGH STEELERS were beating the Dolphins in Miami. Things were going according to plan in Week Six of the 2016 NFL season for the favored Steelers. The tide started to turn, though, halfway through the second quarter. A twenty-three-yard field goal put the Dolphins within one scoring drive of taking the lead for the second time in the game.

On the Steelers' next possession after that Miami field goal, quarterback Ben Roethlisberger took the snap and quickly started backward, turning to his left in a fake hand-off attempt. He then rolled out to the right side of the field, moving quickly toward the far sideline while looking to pass downfield.

As Roethlisberger started to move right, Miami defensive tackle Jordan Phillips broke through the Steelers' offensive line and gave chase. Phillips dived at Roethlisberger's legs and managed to momentarily grab Roethlisberger's right foot. Roethlisberger awkwardly stutter-stepped and threw. The less-than-perfect spiral landed in the hands of Miami's Rashad Jones for an interception.

This was bad news for the Steelers for two reasons. First, the Dolphins, already in striking distance of taking the lead, now had possession of the ball and excellent field position. Second, the awkward movement by Roethlisberger as a result of having his right foot grabbed had placed enormous stress on his left knee. He limped a bit as he walked off the field after the play was over. Later we learned that Roethlisberger had torn his left meniscus, a piece of cartilage in the knee meant to cushion the union between the upper femur bone and the lower tibia bone, during that play. He would need surgery.[1]

Arthroscopic surgery is the typical surgical method for repairing knees with this ailment. This surgery requires opening one or more small holes in the skin around the knee to allow the arthroscope, a small camera, to see the inside. With the camera in place, the doctor can use other specialty tools inserted through other small holes around the knee to complete the work. According to the *New England Journal of Medicine*, arthroscopic partial meniscectomy is the most common orthopedic procedure in the United States, with 700,000 operations performed annually.[2]

Arthroscopic knee surgery is a popular way to reduce knee pain due to meniscus tears, but Roethlisberger might have been just as well-off by having fake surgery. It turns out that alleviating knee pain associated with this type of injury happens when surgery is performed on the knee, and alleviating knee pain also happens when surgery is faked.

In a study of this phenomenon, 146 willing participants were assembled to test the hypothesis that fake surgery could be just as potent as real surgery.[3] Of the 146 patients, 70 were assigned to actual surgery and 76 were assigned to "sham" surgery. The 70 participants assigned to real surgery had actual arthroscopic surgery on their meniscus tissue. The 76 patients assigned to sham surgery had a convincing but simulated surgery. The variables between the groups, like how long they were in the surgical room, were similar.

In essence, the surgeons simulated an actual surgery as closely as possible so that the participants would be unaware of what group they belonged to. The results seem unbelievable.

After rounds of questionnaires in the months after the surgery, the researchers found that participants in both groups experienced improvement. Amazingly, the patients assigned to real surgery had no greater improvement than those assigned to sham surgery. This case study illustrates the power of our expectations.

EXPECTATIONS AND FUTURE GENERATIONS

Expectations, as journalist Chris Berdik notes, have the power to bend reality.[4] Studies have shown that expectations have the power to heal knees, lift depression, and create debilitating side effects from cornstarch pills. The expectation that a drug has the ability to heal—even if there are no active ingredients in that drug—is enough to initiate improvement for many patients. Even symptoms of Parkinson's have been alleviated through the placebo effect.[5] Expectations are powerful. While their presence and their absence plays a powerful role in our health, expectations also play a powerful role in the workplace.

So, let me ask you this: Do you really know what is expected of you at work? And, how do you know what is expected of you? If you are crystal-clear on what's expected from you at work, then you are in mixed company. Research has shown that only half of all employees know what is expected of them. And, this isn't only a problem for the rank-and-file. The same research showed that managers also suffer from unclear expectations. Like the employees they supervise, half of all managers are similarly unclear about what is expected from them at work.[6] The problem is that when expectations are unclear, performance suffers to some degree. The antidote to these performance problems is setting clear expectations.

A Qualtrics-Accel survey of almost 1,500 Millennials identified the top five things Millennials want when they start a new job. Almost a third said that having clear expectations and goals is the second most important thing in a new job (right behind sufficient training).[7] If we read this another way, though, we can see that Millennials are really saying that they want to be in an environment where they can perform at a high level. If they know what is expected, they will then have a better chance at meeting or exceeding those expectations.

As the Millennial representation in the workplace continues to increase, future leaders looking for the keys to high performance will need to evolve their leadership styles to meet the demands of this generation. One way to do this is through setting clear expectations.

SETTING EXPECTATIONS

Setting expectations cannot be done in a vacuum. Expectations, to work properly, have to be attached to a larger mission, and they have to be part of an intentional program. A program of expectations includes creating the expectations, consistently communicating what the expectations are, following-up and providing feedback, and holding people accountable for results. You'll find ideas about creating a program of expectations below.

START WITH A CLEAR MISSION. And we are back once again to the importance of having a clear mission. It is possible to set and follow through on expectations without a mission, but it will be impossible to tie the value of a team member's daily work to a greater purpose without one. That greater purpose helps fuel the motivation to achieve established goals and metrics. If you don't have the mission figured out yet, or the mission is weaker than diner coffee, then there is a problem. Expectations become less motivating in the eyes of top employees if they're not tied to something larger than just making money. Reread Chapter Seven to refresh on creating a clear and compelling mission.

IDENTIFY WHAT YOU WANT. My guess is you want whatever scenario you have in your head to match the scenario that plays out in the workplace. You are looking for production from your people that meets what you imagine they are capable of. But, have you taken the time to clarify exactly what that is? Thinking about success, and clearly articulating to ourselves and others what it looks like, is the leadership stuff we get paid to do. In addition, clarifying what you are looking for in creating a program of expectations will help guide the rest of the program's development.

OUTLINE THE EXPECTATIONS PROGRAM. Setting expectations won't work if we just summon somebody and give them a list of stuff to do with a due date. Instead, future leaders should look to create a holistic program that involves both the technical aspects and aspirational elements of creating a new program. The technical elements are the how the program is structured. The aspirational elements tie the expectations to something larger.

On the technical side, you will want to identify a few elements of the program. First, how will you set expectations for your team, and how will you communicate those expectations? Identify if the communication will happen through one-on-one meetings, team meetings, email, or some other way. Whatever method you select, you don't have to stick with it forever. The method of communication may change, but the consistency of communicating the expectations shouldn't.

Second, identify how much time you will allocate to this new program on a weekly basis? Leadership cannot be squeezed into the five minutes you have left on a Thursday evening. Rather, this is one of those leadership activities that will require regular workday time and attention. You will need a certain amount of time to think about and create the expectations in the first place. You will need the time to communicate those expectations. You will need the time each week to follow up and hold people accountable. What windows of time can you set aside each week for this new program?

Third, what is your plan for holding people accountable? Accountability is not only tied to not meeting expectations, but also happens when expectations are met. How can you celebrate someone when their performance meets or exceeds the expectation? Conversely, how can you gently help someone correct their course if they are getting derailed? Don't wing it with accountability in the moment. Think it out ahead of time.

On the aspirational side, identify how the expectations help the team or the organization succeed toward its mission. We talked in Chapter Eight about creating stories from data. This is a similar concept. As the future leader, you will be rewarded for connecting the daily work to the mission with higher team engagement and performance. How can you weave the daily work and the larger mission together into a story that becomes sticky? How can you communicate it to your people in a way that motivates and inspires them?

To enjoy long-term success with the skill of setting expectations means building a dedicated program. By doing so, the program becomes something that will not be set aside when things inevitably become busy. Understand that creating a program of expectations for your organization or team means you will need to build time into your schedule every week.

SET OR REESTABLISH THE EXPECTATION AROUND EXPECTATIONS. Once you have outlined what your program of expectations looks like and how it will function, then it is time to reset the team. Creating a program of expectations, like other organizational initiatives, will require buy-in on some level. If a program around expectations will be new to your organization, or if you are new to setting expectations, or if the process of setting expectations has grown stale in your organization, then start by doing a hard reset.

People don't like being broadsided with a new work "thing" out of the blue. Provide a proper heads-up on what you are working on and what it will eventually look like. More transparency is a good thing and promotes trust. A heads-up will give people time to think about and warm to the idea, and may help implementation go a bit smoother. Too much communication is not possible when it comes to making workplace changes.

BE UNCOMFORTABLY CLEAR AND DIRECT WHEN SETTING EXPECTATIONS. After your program has been developed, it's time to get your hands dirty. When setting expectations, don't assume that everyone is clear because likely there is some confusion somewhere yet to be found. The best way I have found to set expectations is to be uncomfortably clear and direct. We aren't trying to make the interaction uncomfortable, but we do need to communicate what we want as clearly and directly as possible. This usually means verbalizing things that may seem obvious. But, what is obvious to me may not be obvious to the person I am talking to.

At one point in the Steven Seagal movie *Under Siege 2: Dark Territory,* the villain says, "Assumption is the mother of all fuck-ups." While not the most elegant line, I do picture that scene in my head and hear that line when assumptions come back to bite me. When we aren't as clear as we should be, assumptions tend to fill in the remaining void. Instead, be uncomfortably clear and direct. The discomfort will fade as you put this into practice and your team members become accustomed to it.

BE ACCESSIBLE. As the leader, there is no reason you should not be accessible on a regular basis. This doesn't mean you have your door open all the time for any disruption, but it does mean you are available on a regular and frequent basis. Being accessible means people feel comfortable showing up at your space and getting your take on issues. The "feeling comfortable" part is really important. A gesture of accessibility is worthless if your team gets the repeated message that interruptions are unwelcome.

Being accessible means you respond to emails in short order, even if to acknowledge that you don't have an answer yet. It means promptly returning phone calls. It means turning your whole body away from the screen to face the person who has stopped by. Being accessible means the team considers you a valuable resource to help make things happen.

PROVIDE REGULAR FEEDBACK, ESPECIALLY TO MILLENNIALS. Your annual performance evaluation (if you still do those) should be a foregone conclusion for the people you lead. They should know exactly where they stand and how well they are doing on any given day. Built into a proper expectations program is regular feedback. The data shows that Millennials prefer even more feedback than other generations, and more feedback than you think.

In a 2014 survey of 1,400 Millennials, the research confirmed that preferences for feedback are distinctly different for this generation than for other generations. About half of the respondents wanted monthly feedback, a rate higher than for other generations.[8] This means there might be a disconnect in your office between how much feedback you are providing, and how much feedback your people want. We can help narrow this gap by incorporating feedback into our expectations program.

OFFER PRAISE FOR MEETING OR EXCEEDING EXPECTATIONS, AND OFFER ACCOUNTABILITY FOR MISSING EXPECTATIONS. Accountability makes our pits sweat and our heartbeats speed up. Somebody has fallen short of the expectation and needs to be held accountable. It sounds harsh. But, it could also be that your team members are performing well and have met or exceeded the expectations. You owe it to the people who move the organization forward to be straight about how things are going, whether good or bad. Praise and celebrate when expectations are met or exceeded. Or, be clear that performance is falling short and find a path forward. Like with setting expectations, be clear and direct. Temper the "falling short" conversations by being kind.

For those who are falling short, try becoming more curious. Ask questions about what is going on. It could be that something was unclear in the first place. It could be that something outside of work is distracting. It could be that your expectations were too high to begin with. Holding someone accountable doesn't have to be an adversarial conversation. Instead, use it as an opportunity to learn.

REGULARLY FOLLOW UP. A key element to a program of expectations is following up with your team on their progress. Too many leaders are there at the beginning of a project and then disappear until the end. Instead, make sure to regularly check in with your team along the way. This may happen in your one-on-one meetings. It may happen via email. It may happen at impromptu times. It may be some combination of methods. The point with checking in is that we want to our team member to be successful. They have a better chance at becoming successful if we are checking in along the way.

USE THE FEEDBACK FROM YOUR TEAM TO ADJUST HOW YOU CREATE EXPECTATIONS. Over time, you will gain a sense for how well the team performs in certain areas. You will also hear from them on how things are going during your follow-up meetings. Use this information to influence how you go about setting expectations in the future.

LAST WORD ON EXPECTATIONS

With Ben Roethlisberger out for the rest of the football game after he tore the meniscus in his left knee, the Steelers couldn't get back on track. They ended up losing to the Dolphins, 30-15. I wonder if part of the reason for the loss was a change of expectations. Did the reality of losing their franchise quarterback in the second quarter create an expectation that the rest of the game would be tough? I can't say, but I do know that expectations are powerful.

In the Future Leadership Framework, creating a program for expectations is a critical skill. Expectations have the ability to magically heal physical injury, and they have the ability to help your staff perform at a consistently high level. People crave some way to keep score at work. Setting and communicating clear expectations can help them do that. Give them that gift.

KEY IDEA

Creating a program that consistently sets expectations, clearly communicates and follows up on those expectations, and holds people accountable for results will serve to increase the engagement and performance of your staff. The future leader creates expectations that align with the team's mission which aligns with the organization's mission.

KEY DIFFERENCES

Yesterday's Leader

Doesn't consistently set expectations
Disjointed expectations effort
Inadvertently makes assumptions

The Future Leader

Regularly sets clear expectations
Creates a program for expectations
Consciously assumes very little

KEY QUESTION

If I came into your office and asked each member of your team if they knew what was expected of them, could they convincingly answer me?

16

Teams

HARNESS THE POWER OF FUTURE TEAMS

As I write this, the house across the street from us is getting its roof replaced. The original builders decided against splurging for plywood under the roofing materials as is customary, so the roofing company, in addition to replacing the old wood shakes with new asphalt shingles, is installing plywood sheets.

What came to mind as I have been watching this work unfold is how the roofing company is approaching the project. For the demolition part of the work, there were four people up on the roof removing the old wood shakes and other materials. After a few days, I saw two people break off from the demolition work to start hammering on new plywood sheets. Before the plywood installation was complete, I saw bundles of new roofing materials being delivered by a company delivery driver and staged on the roof. Yesterday there were two people pneumatically hammering on the new roof shingles.

What's interesting to me about this work in light of this chapter is why this roofing company has created a team for this project in the first place.

WHY CREATE A TEAM IN THE FIRST PLACE?

Why would any company assemble and use a team? This roofing company could be a one-person operation. In a one-person roofing company, the owner would have to complete every task related to running the company including the marketing, signing contracts, site preparation, demolition, materials purchases and delivery, installation, and invoicing. In this configuration, the owner would never have to pay other people. Why not operate the company in this way?

Seattle-area roofing companies have a problem with the seasons. Roofing is, at best, a two-season activity in the Pacific Northwest due to the rain. Summer is prime time for roofing companies, but they can also work for part of spring and part of fall. While the climate of the Pacific Northwest creates pressure to complete roofing projects quickly, schedule pressure alone still doesn't necessitate creating a team to do the work. A sole-owner software company who won't have seasonal pressure, but who will have schedule pressure, could just choose to do fewer projects. There has to be something else tugging at the owner to want to bring on help. I suggest this "tug" is an innate understanding of the concept of division of labor.

The division of labor is a concept credited to Adam Smith, author of *Wealth of Nations.*[1] The idea is that by taking a large job and dividing it up, the assigned staff have an opportunity to become increasingly efficient in their tiny piece of the overall project. Each team member learns how to do their piece of work much faster. This increase in efficiency means the overall project can be done faster, which means that the company can accept and complete more jobs per unit of time. If your organization is for-profit, this equates to earning more money.

Organizations create teams because teams are more efficient.

Teams are also more effective. For-profit and not-for-profit organizations both have a stake in becoming more effective. While it may have been fashionable at some point for companies to have Gordon Gekko-esque instincts when it comes to profitability, the landscape of business is changing. The most skilled talent found in future generations have shown they aren't necessarily motivated by the same things as the skilled talent from the older generations. Millennials are not necessarily all about the Benjamins. Generation Z coming up behind them, as best we can tell, are also not primarily motivated by money. Please don't misunderstand: Future generations are interested in making money, but Millennials and those in Generation Z haven't shown a widespread drive to make money at the expense of other values.

In the new world of work, effectiveness will be measured against how well the organization is executing on its mission. Teams help organizations better execute on their missions, which then helps the organizations become more effective.

For the roofing company, having the right team assembled frees up time for the owner to do other profit-producing activities. For instance, if the owner was able to specialize and focus on business development, then the roofing crews will ultimately move more efficiently from one job to the next. More efficient moves mean less downtime. Less downtime means more revenue and, hopefully, more profit.

OLD TEAMS

Think about the progression of an organization. Many start with only a few people (or just a single person) trying to execute on an idea, awash in the romance of being a "startup." In these early organizations, the team is the whole organization—everybody helps do everything. The organization is small and flat. As the organization begins to succeed on its mission and time becomes tighter for the existing staff, the team will bring in additional people and technology to create more time. If the organization's mission is to be executed at scale, it will need more people.

Scale is the primordial ooze that the traditional, pyramidical organizational structure crawls out from. As the organization grows its labor force, the leadership will naturally segment job responsibilities to create efficiencies.

The old model has been to divide the labor into different functional areas, or verticals. So, the accounting department would be in this corner, engineering would be in a different corner, customer service would be over there, human resources would be on the second floor, and so on. Each vertical then gets its own leadership and management team to coordinate the work of the group in the organization and lead the team. The pyramid continues to grow as new layers of managers and directors are added to the existing verticals. The pyramid structure has a single CEO at the top and successive layers of responsibility filtering down the sides to the massive front-line staff who occupy the flat plane at the bottom of the pyramid.

Functional organizations—those that are split distinctly into accounting, customer service, engineering, etc.—represent a fading model. Only about a third of all companies are functionally organized today, and only about a quarter of large companies are set up this way.[2] Deloitte's Global Human Capital Trends 2016 report noted that well over three-quarters of organizations have recently restructured or are currently restructuring. Only 7 percent responded that they have no plans to restructure.[3]

The only reason to restructure an organization is to improve its performance. Organizations are not only responding to market pressures to get their product out the door quicker, but they also want to foster an empowered culture, which they believe comes from smaller teams.[4] And, the trend now has the technological foundation to make reorganization work. Deloitte says, "Teams can easily use web or mobile apps to share goals, keep up-to-date on customer interactions, communicate product quality or brand issues, and build a common culture."[5] Better technology means we can get information faster, instead of waiting for information to filter up and down the corporate pyramid. Getting information faster means we can act on that information much faster as well.

The problem with the traditional corporate pyramid combined with functional work groups is agility. Bigger organizations simply can't move fast enough to respond to market conditions. McKinsey notes that: "Large and established companies often become bureaucratic because the rules, policies, and management layers developed to capture economies of scale ultimately hamper their ability to move fast."[6] And speed is key. While an S&P 500 company in the 1950s had an average life span of sixty years, S&P 500 companies today are only averaging about fifteen-year life spans. Deloitte notes that: "Lean start-ups are moving with purpose, speed, and agility to reshape markets. By contrast, most major corporations are heavily layered, bureaucratic, and stifled by complex webs of reporting lines that weigh down leadership and smother talent."[7] Speed is how organizations are responding to the current market conditions.

The problem is not necessarily the structure of a single CEO followed by layers of management and front-line staff, rather it's the number of layers and the composition of the organization's teams in the overall structure. The combination of more layers and functionally organized departments creates silos that naturally slow decision-making and information flow. As organizations remove layers, communication and decision-making speed up, and time spent on information coordination decreases.[8] The increasing need for agility coupled with fewer layers dictate a change to how teams are conceived and structured.

Many organizations have already changed their approach to teaming in light of market conditions. An iteration on the functional team is the cross-functional team. The cross-functional teams of today evolved from yesteryear's matrix organizations. In a matrix organization, members from different functional areas would be assigned to projects with project managers. These employees would not leave the functional department they belonged to, but they would be assigned to a new project with people from other departments. In its simplest iteration, the team members essentially reported to two supervisors—the department supervisor and the project manager. The cross-functional teams of today are similar in that people from different disciplines are assembled into teams depending on the projects at hand. The concept of the cross-functional team is moving in the right direction, but still lags behind the teams of the future.

FUTURE TEAMS

The successful future organization will be structured to leverage efficiencies that come from smaller, more nimble, and distributed teams with clear lines of communication, clear objectives, and active accountability. These teams may consist solely of organization employees, but many teams will likely have members from outside shops for specialty roles. Organizations will continue to flatten by removing layers of management. As these layers disappear, the responsibility for coordination and control will shift from the management layer to the teams and the team leaders. These teams will necessarily act more like tight-knit individual pods within a larger shell than loose assemblies of people that work together on occasion. Future teams will liaise with other teams for organizational resources, and to collect and transmit information.

The power source of the future team is technology.

With the advent of good, reliable, and cheap video conferencing, web-based applications, and mobile production, teams can have members working from different ZIP codes. A number of organizations already have teams with members in different locales around the world—a distributed team—and this trend will continue. A free account on Zoom or Skype helps team members communicate easily across town or across time zones. Web-based applications can handle document flow and version control and can help teams better manage projects. Tools like Asana, Basecamp, Google Docs, and Office 365 will continue to help future teams collaborate.

Production mobility means work can be completed anywhere, not just in the office at the desktop computer. Use of laptops and tablets and smartphones help our "offices" become mobile.

Technology, though, is not being fully leveraged. This will change as tech continues to improve. Distributed teams are not created because it's sexy to have people working all over the world. Rather, the organizations who build these types of teams are looking for skilled talent wherever these talented people reside. At one time, our organizations could only attract skilled workers who were within a certain commute to the physical offices, now that talent can log into the virtual private network from wherever they reside around the world.

The same technology that will be powering distributed teams of employees will also usher in a new era of partnering with outside organizations. Technology that allows an employee to work anywhere around the world is also powering entrepreneurs to start their own small shops. There is no rule saying your organization can't partner with outside companies to provide expertise or fill a hole on a team. If you have an architectural company and need drafting help on a certain project, why not partner with somebody who runs a small shop instead of hiring an employee?

This isn't a new or novel concept. What is different, though, will be the availability and accessibility of these small-shop practitioners as opposed to large companies, and the economies that can be captured by hiring small shops or individual practitioners. Solo practitioners usually don't have the overhead of the larger companies, which means potential cost savings. A solo drafter working out of a home office in Oklahoma City will likely not charge the same fee as a drafting company based in a downtown San Francisco skyscraper.

The concept of developing a bench of talent will be critical. Having relationships with a variety of small-shop practitioners who can assist puts your team, and your organization, at a competitive advantage. But this advantage will require building those relationships in the first place. The problem will not be finding warm bodies to outsource work to, it'll be finding and scheduling work with the best small shops. The best are typically busy. But if you have developed a relationship, there is a better chance that the busy shop will help you when needed.

If the idea of leading a widely distributed team that may be constructed of far-flung employees and contractors seems daunting, it's because it is—at least in comparison to leading a historically composed team. While organizations can still create a group of employees in a central location to work on projects, they don't have to. And that is the point of all of this. The generations coming up in the workplace now, coupled with advancing technology, are changing expectations and possibilities. If the company is truly mission-driven, then the mission will drive decision-making. It might feel good to have a centrally located team in cubicles just outside or your office, but is it the best configuration for executing the mission? If so, great! If not, then something needs to change, and that "something" might be the organization's comfort level.

IDEAS FOR BUILDING BETTER TEAMS

ASSESS YOUR TEAM'S EFFECTIVENESS IN ITS CURRENT COMPOSITION. Most of us are likely working with teams that are already established. But, we want to understand what the structure of the team could look like so we know how to approach rebuilding the team when people eventually move on.

The question going forward is: Where is this team weak? If you were assessing your team for effectiveness with respect to its mission, where is the team deficient? Understanding where the weakness is means you are better poised to make alternate decisions about team composition over time.

KEEP THE TEAMS AS SMALL AS POSSIBLE. Smaller teams that have adequate access to resources and support, and smaller teams with real decision-making authority, can be faster to market than their lumbering counterparts. You may have heard of the two-pizza rule at Amazon—that teams should be small enough to be fed by two pizzas.[9] Participant engagement and production tends to go up as the teams become smaller. Everybody knows, or can know, what everybody else is working on. As the teams grow bigger, there are more places to hide. Intentionally structure your teams to be as small as possible.

MAKE YOUR TEAM STICKIER. As the future leader, you want to make your teams as sticky as possible. Meaning, you want to attract the right people, whether as employees or as external teaming partners, and then you want them to stick around. With the right team members in the right environment, team cohesion and natural synergies are likely to improve. Synergies are really helpful in the "do more with less" environment we all seem to find ourselves in.

Making your team as sticky as possible is a multi-faceted effort. It comes from having and communicating a clear mission, and organizing team-building and social events. It comes from your emotional intelligence. The particular tactics to create this stickiness will be unique for each team, but the goal of keeping the best people on your team is the same.

UNDERSTAND THAT TEAM MEMBERS WILL LIKELY BE ON MORE THAN ONE TEAM. The agility required in the future organization will mean team members will likely be on more than one team. They might be on the compensation committee as well as on your team. They might be on the annual event steering committee, or the holiday party planning committee, or a strategic planning team, or other project teams. For future leaders, this comes back to the skills of emotional intelligence and empathy. Your people will continue to be pulled in a number of directions. How will this reality affect how you lead your team?

ENSURE THE TEAM IS CLEAR. Teams are always assembled for a specific purpose. Whatever that purpose is for your team, it should directly relate to the organization's mission. I know, this sounds basic, but from what I have seen it's worth repeating. The purpose might be short-term or ongoing, but the team members ought to be crystal clear on what the purpose of the team is, why it is important, and how it relates to the mission of the organization. If the team is new, then the perfect time to ensure this clarity is at a kickoff meeting. If the team has been assembled for some time, then there is no harm in rehashing the purpose in the next staff or status meeting. In either case, you will want to ensure that at points along the way, the team remains clear about the overall objective and purpose of the team. This can be accomplished individually if you feel a team member is straying, or it can be done as an appendix to an already established meeting.

ESTABLISH TEAM GOALS AND METRICS. With a clear understanding of the overall goal and purpose of the team, the next question is: What does success look like? If the organizational leadership has been carefully communicating the larger strategies and the mission and vision of the organization, and the team members understand the mission of the team, then relevant goals and key performance indicators can be created. We talked about key performance indicators in Chapter Nine. Goals should be created by the whole team to help achieve buy-in. The goals should have clear and relevant metrics attached so that team members can see whether they are advancing, treading water, or retreating. Clear metrics also provide data to others outside of the team about progress and efficacy. Using the Future Leadership Framework skill of Synthesis to create stories will help put the metrics into context.

LEVERAGE TECH TO BUILD HUMAN CONNECTION. With team members possibly being located all around the world, creating team cohesion takes on new importance. If the only connection among teammates is via email, then there is room for improvement. Use video conferencing to bring people virtually into the same room. Maybe there is an annual retreat where all the team members gather for a few days. Talk on the telephone so you can hear the team members' voices. Voices tell stories if you listen to more than the words. Using technology to leverage human connection within teams will help increase stickiness and empathy among the team members.

FIND OUTSIDE PEOPLE TO TEAM WITH AHEAD OF NEEDING THEM. Depending on what projects your team is working on, you may need to develop a bench of outside contracted help. Look to smaller shops that can keep overhead low, instead of large, established companies. These are easier to find now than ever before. Find that one person who really does a technical task well, and develop the relationship. You are looking for long-term partners here, not disposable help on an immediate project. With a strong bench of talent inside and outside the organization, movement toward the goals of the team, and ultimately toward the mission of the organization, will improve.

CHANGE PERSONNEL WHEN NEEDED. Professional football teams don't keep everybody around year after year. The Seahawks—my home team—make roster changes regularly. I don't think organizations do this enough. We tend to let the 70-percenters hang around for way too long. The 70-percenters don't have a chance with the Seahawks. A player is either playing at 100 percent or he is moved along. Sometimes even the 100-percenters are moved along. To be sure, most organizations are different than football teams, but the concept translates. Do you have anyone underperforming on your team? What have you done to address this team member's underperformance?

Ultimately, we want to match up great people with the right work. Sometimes we incorrectly match people with jobs. It doesn't mean the person is bad, it just means the match isn't right. Do everything reasonable to help bring everyone up to or above standard, and make sure to properly address underperformance.

LAST WORD ON TEAMS

The hardest part about all of this will be grasping the level of change required by our leaders when it comes to future teams. The business landscape for future organizations will require leaders to be agile such that the team is producing despite distractions caused by a work environment that is being stressed by generational churn and rapid technological advancement. This means future leaders may want to consider adopting an attitude of experimentation—an attitude of, let's try it, see how it works, tweak it, try again, and so on. Many people don't like working this way. It feels too loose. But, there will often be a difference between what feels right and what is actually right. As a future leader, you will be required to regularly work in your discomfort zone.

KEY IDEA

Building the right teams creates divisions of labor that allow an organization to effectively make progress toward its mission. Understanding the power of teams, future leaders will leverage rapidly advancing technology to find the most skilled talent wherever those people reside. These future teams may be composed of in-house employees, remote employees, outside small-shop contractors, or some combination of the three.

KEY DIFFERENCES

Yesterday's Leader

Sticks with functional teams
Wants people assembled in one place
Relies on people inside the organization

The Future Leader

Looks to leverage future teams
Wants the best talent wherever they live
Builds a bench of talent inside and outside the organization

KEY QUESTION

In light of this chapter, how should your teams be structured to best make progress toward the mission?

17

Training

GROW YOUR GREATEST ASSET

YOU KNOW THAT FEELING when something sounds really good while the plans are being made, but then once you get into it, you wonder what you were thinking? Several years ago, on the morning of the fourth day of instruction for an industry training certification, I had that distinct feeling. The training seemed straightforward when I signed up. I would fly to Dallas, Texas, for five weekdays of classroom instruction followed by a proctored test on Saturday. No problem. I had attended industry trainings and conferences in the past. This one was different. The printed modules that were sent to me after I signed up indicated there would be a lot of information to digest in a short time. After briefly thumbing through the materials, I set them aside. I picked them up again when I was packing for the flight.

On the first morning, the instructor confirmed my suspicion. "If you are coming into this training cold, you won't succeed," he said. I couldn't tell if he was kidding. "Hopefully, you have been studying the modules we sent you ahead of time." Oops. He then shared some of his own data he had collected about how well people did who were unprepared. It was not encouraging. During the week I pushed through the material in marathon sprints, but being in constant overdrive caught up to me by Thursday morning. I was burning out and I was having serious doubts about my ability to pass the upcoming test.

When the subject of training comes up, this is the story I return to. The point of the story is not how difficult this particular training was, but why training is important in the first place. What I learned that week improved my technical skills for my job, but it also helped to improve a number of other skills outside of work. And that is the point. The best training not only improves our technical skills, but also helps us grow as people.

The best part about training is that the downsides are limited while the upsides can last a career.

Think about it. If you attend a bad training session you have squandered the hard costs of the time and money spent on attending, plus the opportunity costs of not doing something else. These downsides are unfortunate, but not the end of the world. Juxtapose that with a great training opportunity. Training that hits the mark is worth the time and money spent, it's worth the missed opportunity cost, and it may continue to pay dividends for years to come.

The focus of training for the future organization should not simply be on improving a certain skillset, it should be focused on helping people reach their individual potentials.

TRAINING IS THE NEW BLACK

As organizations invest in their employees, the employees are more likely to invest in the organization. And while not all leaders can immediately grasp the business case for training in general, the trend lines for investing in training opportunities are moving in the right direction.

Training Magazine reports that training expenditures in the United States in 2015 increased 14.2 percent to almost $71 billion.[1] Spending on outside products and services for training has also radically increased, to about $8 billion, and spending on other training expenditures like renting facilities, buying equipment, and travel has reached almost $29 billion.[2]

The Association for Talent Development reports that spending on employee training has increased to an average of $1,252 per employee in 2015, up from $1,229 per employee in 2014.[3] Organizations are spending more now on training than ever before. The data show that while investment is rising, and training opportunities are increasing, these increases may still not be enough to satisfy the demands of future generations.

Training Millennials Pays Off

The latest research shows that 87 percent of Millennials consider training and development to be an important part of their job.[4] In fact, the desire for training may be the most important difference between the Millennial generation and the older generations.[5] If an organization is looking to attract the most skilled Millennial talent, reviewing its training program should be at the top of its list. Almost six in ten Millennials have cited ongoing learning and growth as extremely important considerations when it comes to a potential new job.[6] One recent survey on the importance of training found that more than two-thirds of UK workers have switched jobs due to limited training opportunities, and nine in ten of these UK workers want their employers to make more training available.[7]

Remember the boredom statistic from Chapter Two? Over 40 percent of Millennials have reported being bored at work. To help keep boredom at bay, future leaders will want to create an environment that offers regular opportunities to learn and improve. Millennials think that training and development is important, and they have the influence to make organizations pay attention.

If we consider this topic in light of the changing workplace demographic, then a new sense of urgency emerges. As Boomers continue to retire over the next decade, and as the available workforce continues to tighten, organizations will naturally skew younger. We know that Millennials are turning twenty-one at a rate of 10,000 per day through 2022.[8] We also know that Millennials will represent half of the overall workforce in just over a year, and up to 75 percent of the workforce by 2025.[9] Millennials have no problem voting with their feet if our organizations are not adapting fast enough.

We saw in a previous chapter that the average employee tenure for Millennials right now is less than three years. Organizations have a choice about whether to offer training opportunities, but skilled Millennials also have the choice about whether to work for you. This might sound harsh, but we are in an unabashed employees' market. Recently, an article with the subtitle "America has more jobs than ever before" reported that some 6 million jobs are open across the country.[10] With so many unfilled jobs, there is a serious imbalance in the supply and demand of skilled talent such that those with in-demand skills now have the upper hand. Organizations looking to attract top-tier skilled Millennial talent would be wise to establish a robust training program as a perk of employment.

A perk of employment? We might be on to something here.

TRAINING AND DEVELOPMENT REBOOTED

The 1989 Batman movie starring Michael Keaton had my attention. It was dark and weird and funny. The Batman movies that followed missed the mark for me. By the time the bat-nipples appeared in the Val Kilmer edition of *Batman Forever*, I was lost. The 2005 reboot, *Batman Begins*, by director Christopher Nolan restored my hope in the Caped Crusader. Training for a number of organizations feels like it has taken a similar route. It started off good, then at some point it dipped. Now, training is poised for a reboot and a resurgence.

To reboot something means starting over with its essence and then making it new. A reboot adapts the basic concept to the current times. I suggest future organizations reboot their programs to make training a perk of employment.

Turn Training Into a Perk of Employment

Just saying the word "perk" makes us smile. Who doesn't like getting something extra for free? If you are a skilled tech worker in Silicon Valley, you can expect good job perks.[11] At Google, that internal pull for a bit of shut-eye in the midafternoon can be accommodated in a nap pod. At the software company Asana, new employees are given $10,000 to furnish their workspace. Spend the money on whatever you like. Twitter offers its employees unlimited vacation. Other companies offer Ping-Pong tables, cafés with free food at all times of day, on-site healthcare, and other services to enhance quality of life. The Bill & Melinda Gates Foundation has recently extended paid parental leave to one year for new parents as a benefit of employment.[12]

Perks like these aren't the norm. Leaders in more traditional work environments may see these perks as money ill-spent, especially if the organization offering the perks is "pre-profit." "How can a company that has yet to turn a profit justify spending money on lavish perks?" It's a fair observation, but perks serve a purpose.

Superficially, perks serve to attract skilled and scarce talent to the organization. The kind of talent that powers Silicon Valley companies worth millions or billions of dollars is relatively hard to find. Perks can make a company more attractive to potential new hires, and their absence can also make a company less attractive. Fundamentally, though, perks serve to improve an employee's quality of life and help create a new baseline for everyday living.

What if we took that concept of perks and applied it to training? What if leaders used training opportunities to help improve their employee's quality of life? We know that the next generation of workers overwhelmingly values access to training and development, but what if organizations took it a step further and offered training outside of what has been traditionally offered? Like perks, we can take the concept of training to the next level and offer opportunities for our employees not only to improve their work skillsets, but to improve their life. This is training rebooted.

A rebooted training program will still offer the core types of training that help people improve the hard or soft skills associated with their jobs. Training for hard skills would include technical training on new software programs, compliance procedures, or safety procedures, while training for soft skills may include leading teams, giving feedback, setting clear expectations, coaching employees, improving customer service, and more. These are a great start, but there are other opportunities.

Other opportunities may include bringing in a fitness trainer to work with a small group of employees in the building's gym, training them on how to use the equipment, creating proper workouts, and answering questions. Maybe the organization offers a cooking demonstration in its café of healthy and easy-to-prepare dinners for busy people. What if there was a seminar that taught employees the basics of investing (not offered by the partial 401k provider)?

These are just a few ideas to get creativity flowing. The underlying concept, though, is what's important. An organization can reboot its existing training program to make it more like a perk of employment.

This kind of reboot is already in its infancy at a number of organizations, we just call it something else. A 2017 survey of 141 companies by The National Business Group on Health reports that more than a third of companies offer mindfulness training classes up from 22 percent in 2016.[13] In addition, 40 percent of companies either had or planned to have resiliency training programs in 2017, up from 27 percent in 2016.[14] They have been labeled "wellness programs" but at their core, they are training programs. While a result of these particular opportunities is an improved quality of life, these training programs also benefit the bottom line.

Training programs also help boost employee engagement. For instance, research done by Quantum Workplace shows that employee engagement scores improved by over 5 percent as a direct result of having an onsite nutritionist.[15] If your training program increases engagement, that may help lower the rate of turnover and increase productivity.

IDEAS TO IMPROVE TRAINING AND DEVELOPMENT

If you are looking to reboot your training program to make it more like a perk of employment, then consider the following ideas.

GET CLEAR ON THE OVERALL GOAL OF YOUR TRAINING PROGRAM. What is the purpose of your training and development program? What are you hoping the training program will accomplish? Is it about attracting high-skilled talent in a tight job market? Is it about employee retention? Is it about reducing risk? Don't overlook this step as a clear goal will help to inform what the overall training program looks like, how much investment it should have, and how it is rolled out.

GET CREATIVE WHEN EVALUATING RETURN ON INVESTMENT. If your organization pays someone $250 to come in and do a half-day seminar on using the building's gym, then you should have some method to track the return on investment. The return in this case might be employee happiness, and the measurement might come from a periodic employee survey that seeks to capture the effectiveness of the training programs (among other things).

The key to understanding any training opportunities' return on investment is to have a consistent way to measure the effectiveness of the program. So, if one of your measurement metrics is turnover, then you should be measuring turnover over time with due consideration to all of the variables that go into this figure (clear mission, employee connection, pay, training, job matching, etc.). Consistent measurement is the only way to gauge whether any training program creates an appropriate ROI.

LEADERS NEED BUY-IN FROM ALL LEVELS OF MANAGEMENT. Future leaders creating a rebooted training program of any variety will need to sell the concept up and down the organization. This means the future leader will need to refine the business case for the training reboot. Think about the structure of the program, about its potential cost, and about its potential benefits. If buy-in is missing at the outset, then the program simply won't work.

TREAT THE REBOOT AS AN EXPERIMENT. None of what you create has to be cast in concrete. To discover the elements of a rebooted training program that work may mean trying a number of ideas and gauging what resonates with the staff. Like most of the skills in the Future Leadership Framework, creating a training program will be an iterative process. Adopt an attitude of experimentation when it comes to your training program.

CLARIFY THE DETAILS. Training programs will vary greatly depending on how large your organization is. One program may work really well in an organization of fifty people, but may be too onerous in an organization of five hundred. The questions are: What are you looking to achieve with this training program? And, how can you make this training program work well for your organization? For every training opportunity, there should be some thought about its structure, when it is offered, its goal, and who it's intended for. Not all programs are suitable for all employees, nor should they be. Training rebooted is training customized for the organization, or for teams within the organization.

ENSURE THE REBOOTED PROGRAM FOCUSES ON MORE THAN JOB SKILLS. We talked about this above, but it's worth repeating here. For the future organization, the goal of training and development is not only to help someone get better at their job, but to help them reach their individual potential. Offering job skills training is important, but also offering learning and development opportunities outside of strict job skills is critical to the reboot.

BUDGET DIFFERENTLY FOR TRAINING AND DEVELOPMENT. Organizations have budgets, and if they have training and development programs, they are typically in the budget as a line item. While this general structure is fine, how we think about allocating funds to that line item may need an update. I would suggest making the total line item a multiple of head count. Meaning, instead of setting a static budget for training expenses, the budget instead reflects the head count in the organization. So, in this scenario, the organization attaches training dollars to each team member it hires. Like a 401k match, or health benefits, training becomes a part of the overall pay package. This means that the training budget may need to be more fluid than it currently is to keep pace with additional hires. It also means that training may become more of an organizational focus than it might have been up until now. Once real money is attached to each team member, training will get its due attention.

COMMUNICATE THE LARGER GOAL OF THE TRAINING PROGRAM. Don't assume that team members will make connections on their own. Tell them what the program is and why it is important. Explain that the organization wants to actively invest in its people, and that the focus is personal improvement, not just business improvement. We want to create a strong mental association in the minds of our staff that this organization cares about their long-term development. Reinforce the message often.

TRAINING OPPORTUNITIES CAN BE OUTSOURCED. Not all training has to take place on-site. Starbucks outsourced a facet of its training to Arizona State University.[16] Though not required, employees can choose to pursue a college degree from ASU as a perk of employment. Employees can then fit their education around their work schedules. As you are creating or rebooting the training program for your organization, explore outside opportunities for training that your organization might participate in.

TRAIN FOR TECHNOLOGY. Consider getting your staff up-to-speed on the software applications that will affect their lives—both at work and in their personal lives. Go wide with this approach. Maybe you want to move your company or your team onto Instagram to find more customers, so you find an Instagram course that will help your people become more effective on the platform. Despite our preconceptions about future generations, not every younger person is an Instagram pro. Maybe you bring someone in to talk about how AI is changing your industry and what can be expected in the years ahead.

MAKE SURE TO ASK AROUND. Nobody says you have to come up with any of this in a vacuum. Survey your team members to find out what interests them. What areas, related to work, are most appealing? What technical skills could they use a refresher on? What soft skills would they be most interested in? Ask them about learning opportunities outside of their day-to-day tasks. What have they always wanted to learn more about? Offer up some ideas to get the creative energy up. This can be done simply, and for free, with a program like SurveyMonkey, or it can be done in your one-on-one meetings.

CREATE A SCHEDULE FOR TRAINING IN ADVANCE. Consider allocating time to creating a training program each calendar year. The idea is to have the basic outline of the training program created ahead of time. This type of batch processing will reduce your total time investment and should be easier than looking at the program in piecemeal fashion. Probably best not to hold fast to any schedule for training because business conditions warrant a certain amount of flexibility. Also, issues may arise as the year progresses that weren't on your radar when you outlined the initial training program. You'll want to create a basic outline of the training program for the year, but also have the ability to make changes in the moment.

LAST WORD ON TRAINING

To my relief, I did manage to pass the exam on the Saturday after that week of training. More importantly, what I got out of that training has stuck with me for over five years now. We want to attract and retain great people on our team who are engaged and, at the same time, who will continue to grow both professionally and personally. There are more open jobs as of this writing than ever before. The competition among organizations for skilled talent has never been greater than it is right now. One way to attract and retain the next generation of skilled talent is by creating a robust, rebooted training and development program. Research has indicated there is an overwhelming demand for ongoing learning and development opportunities. Organizations that view training from a new perspective can transform outdated training opportunities into something more like company perks—a benefit of employment designed to attract and retain skilled talent.

KEY IDEA

A rebooted training and development program is one way an organization can attract and retain future generations of skilled talent. These training programs should feel more like a perk of employment than the stale training programs of yesteryear. The focus of a rebooted training program should be helping people get better at their job, and helping them reach their individual potential.

KEY DIFFERENCES

Yesterday's Leader

Doesn't understand the value of training
Has not developed a training program
Focuses training solely on technical skills

The Future Leader

Understands the value of training
Creates a customized training program
Focuses training on a variety of skills

KEY QUESTION

How would you rate your training program at attracting and retaining skilled Millennial talent?

18

Organization

ESTABLISH A ROBUST SYSTEM OF ORGANIZATION

THE CAR THAT WAS intentionally abandoned in the Bronx in 1969 sat only ten minutes before a small family came by and removed its radiator and battery. By the end of the day, everything of value had been stripped. Then the car was destroyed. Windows were smashed, other parts were torn off, and the upholstery was ripped.[1]

Another car intentionally abandoned in Palo Alto, California, at the same time went untouched. For more than a week, the Palo Alto car sat without attracting the kind of attention the car in the Bronx did. Then the organizer of this study, Dr. Philip Zimbardo of Stanford University, intentionally hit the Palo Alto car with a sledgehammer to inflict damage. Within hours, vandals also stripped, upended, and destroyed the Palo Alto car.[2]

This could be a story about how people in more affluent areas behave toward others' property as opposed to people in less affluent areas. Instead, this is a story about why vandals destroyed these cars in the first place. Zimbardo was testing a new theory called "Broken Windows," which attempted to describe how crime evolves in a community.

The basic idea of the Broken Windows theory can be

illustrated with an example much closer to home. A few years ago, a new strip-mall type building was being constructed a few cities over from where I live. The building was big and had a huge glass curtain wall on the street-facing side. The construction site had a chain-link fence all around the property.

Driving by one day, I noticed that one of the big front windows had a giant hole. From the hole, cracks in the glass went in every direction. Considering this was an active construction site full of overturned dirt and rocks, likely somebody walking by took the easy opportunity to throw a rock.

I noticed in the following weeks that no one replaced the broken glass. The hole in the window continued to greet the community. It wasn't long before that first hole had company. Vandals threw another rock through the same piece of glass but in a different spot. After the second rock, it seemed the pace of vandalism increased.

One of the ideas from Broken Windows is that untended property has a unique gravitational attraction on people who are out looking for "fun or plunder," even if those people consider themselves to be living on the right side of the law.[3] Although vandals apparently considered the car in the Bronx "untended property" much quicker than vandals in Palo Alto, both communities appear to have ultimately classified both cars as untended property and ultimately destroyed them. The new building, after having one rock thrown through its window, may have also been perceived as untended property and hence vandals threw more rocks through its windows.

Broken Windows Is About More Than Broken Windows

The Broken Windows theory isn't just about broken windows. Rather, it's a way to think about how things happen. In the policing sense, Broken Windows says that serious crime flows from crime that flows from disorder. The founders of this theory noted in their original essay that disorder and crime are linked such that small acts of disorder can evolve into larger crimes.[4] Disorder becomes the seed from which more serious crime grows. But, the theory also says that the reverse is true. Serious crime can be reduced as a by-product of reducing instances of disorder.

If we liberate the Broken Windows theory from its narrow application in policing, the equivalent would be that to fix large problems, we must focus on fixing small problems. For future leaders, one of the best ways to fix small problems is to create a robust system of personal organization.

ORGANIZATION FOR FUTURE LEADERS

Organization, as we talk about it here, is not just about cleaning out your files and your desk drawers and straightening up your workspace. Rather, we're talking about something much more robust. For the future leader, this skill in the Future Leadership Framework is about getting a clear and firm grasp on the work already in progress by you and your team, and on the work that still needs to be done.

Organization helps us become better leaders. Disorganization tends to push us out of the loop on what is happening. If we lose track of where our team is with their work, we lose perspective. If we lose track of we are with our own work, we lose perspective. Disorganization is a problem for many of us right now and its ability to subtly undermine our effectiveness may only grow in the years ahead.

Organization Gets Harder Because Organizations are Flattening

One reason it will get more difficult is that organizations are continuing the longtime trend of flattening. Flattening is the process of removing layers of middle-level management from the organizational chart. When an organization flattens the remaining levels of leadership have a broader span of responsibility and more people reporting to them.

One study that looked at 300 large American firms noted that CEO direct reports almost doubled from four to seven during the 1986 to 1999 study period.[5] The study also noted that positions between the CEO and managers decreased by 25 percent over the same period.[6] The flattening trend is continuing. As of 2012, the number of CEO direct reports continued to climb. Now, the average Fortune 500 CEO has ten direct reports.[7]

Flattening hierarchies and the increase in direct reports are problems not only reserved for CEOs. The trend is pushing down the organization through successive layers of leadership. Just as today's CEO has more direct reports, so do the middle layers of leadership. When spans of control broaden, work inevitably increases. More people and more projects under a single leader necessitate a robust organizational system.

Organization Gets Harder Because We Have More to Do

Additional work that comes from a flattened organization is hard enough, but many leaders are finding that their job responsibilities are being stretched even further. With a concept called "double-hatting," a number of key leaders are assuming projects and roles that are outside of their official jobs.[8] Double-hatting essentially means that today's leaders are not only responsible for a broader span of control, but they are also being tapped for other special projects.

Special projects, and project management in general, are the work of the modern leader. Gone are the days of Frederick Winslow Taylor and his scientific management approach to work. Today's leaders no longer have the luxury of solving problems that relate to breaking apart a standardized work process to make incremental improvements. Instead, today's leaders manage multiple complicated projects, potentially in different verticals. This sentiment is confirmed in a 2015 Work Management Survey that reported that workers today are responsible for managing longer-term projects involving people both inside and outside of the organization.[9] The Work Management Survey found that 94 percent of respondents are managing projects.[10] In essence, many leaders are juggling a number of long-term projects all at different stages of completion that may involve different teams of people and objectives.

The modern leader's changing job duties, coupled with an increased level of authority and responsibility, make it imperative that leaders create a robust and customized system of organization.

And, Disorganization Is Expensive

Another reason in favor of better organization is that the costs of disorganization are high. The office supply company Brother International surveyed almost 800 office workers in 2010 about workplace disorganization. The survey found that we spend about an hour and a half each week just looking for misplaced stuff.[11] If you add it up, we spend almost two weeks every year responding to disorganization.

Brother went on to put these numbers into a broader context. The lost productivity from all this searching costs American companies $89 billion every year.[12] Two-thirds of people from this study spent time looking for misplaced items around their desk or office, and more than half spent time looking for files misplaced on computers. Disorganization wastes time and money.

ORGANIZATION AND THE TWO FORCES

Organization will also become more difficult as a result of the forces of generational churn and rapid technological advancement. Future leaders should expect that their organizations may become unintentionally and temporarily flatter in the years ahead as they scramble to replace retiring talent. This means that future leaders should expect workload increases over and above what they have right now.

In addition, if the current employment tenure for younger generations holds into the future, the future leader could see positions within their broad span of control turning over more often. In this scenario, generational churn would add to the complexity of completing projects on time and on budget. Queue the headache.

Where the force of generational churn may intensify the need of the future leader to create a robust system of organization, the force of rapid technological advancement might prove to be helpful. Software is already on the market that can help leaders access their organization system from anywhere, and many such programs are free to use. Project management software such as Basecamp, Asana, and Trello can connect teams of people within the organization and around the world to an assortment of projects. Documents, conversations, schedules, to-dos, and more can be kept in a single place that can be quickly accessed.

While tech tools can be helpful, future leaders should be cautious about how they're used. With an array of software comes the possibility that team members end up using a variety of solutions that make organization more difficult instead of easier.

If you have not yet created a robust system that tracks all of the tasks and associated projects you and your team are working on, now is the time.

IMPROVING ORGANIZATION

The following are some ideas future leaders can use to help improve the Future Leadership Framework skill of Organization. These strategies won't tell you what tool to use, as that is something each leader should decide for themselves. Rather, these strategies will provide the underlying principles for creating a robust organizational system.

COMMIT TO WRITING IT ALL DOWN. If you don't have everything written down, expect that it will get lost. Allocate some time on a regular basis to simply empty your head of all the items you are tracking at some level but haven't written down. This includes personal and work stuff. Include anything and everything that pops up in your mind as requiring some sort of action or additional thought, from single tasks like "buy new tabs for the car" to projects like "plan for birthday."

This list should include all work projects in your bubble of responsibility, including projects you and other team members are working on. Also include tasks you have delegated to others, along with when you expect to hear back.

If you haven't done this up until now, don't worry about the format of how this gets done yet. A yellow legal pad is probably better than software. We aren't looking for context at this stage, we just want to get the stuff from our heads onto paper.

Warning: if you truly empty your head of everything you are tracking, you will find two things happen. First, your mind will feel a lot freer than it did before you started. Second, you will likely have a very long list of items. Both are normal.

KEEP WHAT YOU HAVE WRITTEN DOWN IN ONE PLACE. One mistake I made early on was using too many different mediums for keeping track of my life: Post-Its, legal pads, whiteboards, my brain, Evernote, Omnifocus, self-sent emails, Word docs, Google docs, scrap paper, desktop hard drive, MacBook air, notes in my wallet, and the reminders app on my iPhone, among other places. Stuff that I was tracking on some level was everywhere and as a result I couldn't find anything. It felt out of control.

If you are writing it all down on paper, keep the papers together. If you are writing it all down on a computer program, keep all of it in one document. Choose one medium, and use it to capture everything.

THINK THROUGH WHAT YOU HAVE WRITTEN DOWN. This is a concept from the book *Getting Things Done* by David Allen, and it is critical.[13] Once the list has been made, it's time to go over what you have written. What exactly did you write down? Are there one-off tasks, such as "buy a monitor," or are your tasks more involved than that? "Plan second-quarter offsite meeting" is a project that likely needs a number of subtasks to be completed first. Is what you have written down a task (one action), or a project (a collection of tasks)? If it's a project, what are the associated tasks you need to complete? The point of thinking through what you have written down is to more completely understand the underlying actions that those tasks and projects require. Distilling large projects down to a collection of tasks makes getting the work done much easier.

LOOK FOR NATURAL WAYS TO CHUNK UP WHAT YOU HAVE WRITTEN DOWN. Where are the natural fault lines in the list you have just created? For sure, chunk your projects with all of their supporting tasks. But you might also chunk in other ways. Maybe you chunk it up depending on whether it's work or personal. Maybe you chunk it up based on the weeks you intend to complete the tasks. Maybe you chunk it up by tasks that could be completed together, such as purchases. For instance, maybe it's possible that one Amazon order could clear up five items on your list. The point is to find some way to segment the items into groups. By doing so, the lengthy list gets context.

USE YOUR CALENDAR. Don't keep appointments, birthdays, vacations, family activities, or anniversaries in your head. Put them all in your calendar. Absolutely no more, "Oh, I forgot it was your birthday today." Each appointment needs to have an appropriate reminder issued with it. For birthdays, it might be three weeks of advance notice. For the weekly staff meeting, the reminder might be only fifteen minutes. Every day, review your calendar. Every. Single. Day. In the morning, review what is happening for the day and the rest of the week.

Some people add tasks as calendar appointments. This never worked for me, but if it works for you I would encourage you to make those appointments.

PURGE REGULARLY. When was the last time you went through your stuff and got rid of the items that were no longer adding value to your life? There is nothing more therapeutic than going through old possessions and shredding them, giving them away, or throwing them out. When you remove the stuff that is not adding value to your life, you instantly make room for all the stuff that is adding value. Likely this will result in a smaller collection of stuff. That's good. Less stuff means each thing you have is just a bit easier to find. But there is a better reason you should consider clearing out the crap.

Researchers at Princeton University found that multiple items in a field of view compete for the brain's resources.[14] If you work in a space that is cluttered, this work environment is stealing slivers of attention from your brain. If you clear the clutter, then improved focus becomes the by-product.

REGULARLY REVIEW AND EVALUATE YOUR SYSTEM AND HOW YOU INTERACT WITH IT. The task and project lists needs to be constantly updated. Items get accomplished. Some items might go away for whatever reason (your partner bought the champagne for this weekend's event already). New items will appear. The master lists will be changing on a daily basis.

The basic question you want to answer is: Is my system still working for me? If so, great. If it needs to be tweaked, that's fine too. Remember, a "good" system is any system that gets used, and a "bad" system doesn't.

SHARE YOUR SYSTEM WITH YOUR TEAM. Organization is a part of Future Leadership Framework because it directly influences your ability to move others to action on a mission. When life is less complicated, we can store the details in a haphazard system. As life begins to get more complex, we need better systems to manage the complexity. If your team members are missing deadlines, missing meetings, and generally give off the vibe that their organizational system is faltering, help them out by sharing what you have created. Your system doesn't have to be perfect before you share it, because it probably never will be perfect. That doesn't mean you can't share the general setup and help others with their organizational systems.

LAST WORD ON ORGANIZATION

A certain liberation happens after you have properly captured every possible project, task, reminder, to-do, and event in a coherent system of organization. Your mind will stop annoying you with reminders (they always come up at times when you can't do anything about them anyway), and it will be easier to focus on the bigger picture. Future leaders, tasked with more information and responsibility in the years to come, will want to invest in creating a robust system of organization.

KEY IDEA

A robust system of organization will help counteract the trends of flattening organizations, broader spans of control, and additional projects. A robust system of organization will also help future leaders more effectively deal with potential unintentional and temporary increases in workload and responsibility as a result of generational churn. More importantly, a better system of organization will allow future leaders to keep tabs on the progress of their teams toward the organization's mission.

KEY DIFFERENCES

Yesterday's Leader

Good but not great system of organization
Only focuses on the big picture
Misunderstands the role of organization

The Future Leader

A robust system of organization
Focuses on details and the big picture
Uses organization to improve effectiveness

KEY QUESTION

Have you created a robust personal organization system that tracks all aspects of your life?

19

SUMMARY

THERE HAS NEVER been a stronger clarion call for leaders who can transition organizations from today to tomorrow than there is right now. Leadership—defined as the ability to move others to action on a mission—is finally bubbling up in our collective consciousness as the best resource to help organizations win in this time of rapid change. The problem is that leadership, as we experience it today, has some problems.

LEADERSHIP ON THE ROCKS

Part of the problem is that leadership in a number of organizations is underperforming. We know this is the case because research has measured the outcomes of leadership, and those outcomes aren't good. Some of the most telling outcomes include:

1. Employee engagement numbers that are startlingly low;
2. Expectations that are unclear, not communicated, missing, or weak;

3. Feedback that is spare, unhelpful, or missing altogether;

4. A mission that is unclear, not communicated, missing, or weak; and

5. Turnover that is way higher than it needs to be due to burnout and other factors.

Underperforming leadership is not only emotionally expensive, but financially costly as well. Imagine if you added a line item to your organization's yearly budget labeled "Underperforming Leadership." How much has this line item been costing you?

THE FORCE OF GENERATIONAL CHURN

Organizations that are suffering from underperforming leadership are being further agitated by the force of generational churn—the movement of the generations through the workplace.

As the people who make up the generations continue to age, their presence and influence at work continues to change. Boomers are retiring and taking their preferences with them as they leave. The last of the Millennials are turning twenty-one and most of this generation is now in the workforce. The result of this massive changing of the guard is a period of disruption that can create the conditions for chaos, backbiting, irritation, frustration, and turnover.

The work of the future leader when it comes to generational churn will be creating a work environment that continues to advance toward its mission despite the friction.

THE FORCE OF RAPID TECHNOLOGICAL ADVANCEMENT

The force of generational churn is not the only force agitating our organizations. The second force is rapid technological advancement. This is advancing technology that is changing what we do and how we do it.

At this point in our technological timeline, the work of the future leader will not be continuing to find better, cheaper, and faster digital solutions to every analog problem. Rather, it will be discerning what technology, implemented in which way, best helps the organization execute its mission. This is a much different way to look at technology, and a concept many leaders haven't latched on to yet.

THE IDEA

Leaders can win the future by fully leveraging the power of leadership. Creating leverage through leadership requires two actions. First, leaders will need to focus their time, energy, and attention on developing the lead domino skills that will best move other people to action on the organization's mission. Meaning, of all the skills a leader could choose to develop, the leader should focus on skills that will most improve the leadership effectiveness baseline and best respond to the forces of generational churn and rapid technological advancement.

Second, as leaders develop these skills, they will need to spend more time on leadership activities and less time on activities outside of leadership. Most leaders I have come across have both leadership and technical components to their work. They are true working leaders. But, to fully leverage leadership power, these working leaders will need to spend more time on the leadership aspects of their work, and less time on other activities.

The lead domino skills that matter most right now are found in the Future Leadership Framework. This framework promises to improve one's ability to fully leverage leadership considering where leadership is at today, and considering the forces of generational churn and rapid technological advancement.

A FRAMEWORK FOR THE FUTURE OF LEADERSHIP

The Future Leadership Framework groups the lead domino skills into three distinct abilities: Creativity, Interactivity, and Productivity.

As the world continues to speed up, we will desperately need leaders who can find, filter, and respond to the right problems. There will be more problems to solve in the years ahead than there will be resources available, so which ones will get an organization's focus and which won't? This essential question and the skills that help leaders answer this question are grouped under the Creativity ability.

As high-skilled talent becomes harder to attract and retain, we will also need leaders who can convincingly enroll people into the organization and its mission. How can an organization expect to compete in the future economy without having the best people around? It can't. And yesterday's leaders haven't allocated enough time into attracting and retaining the best people.

We can no longer bark orders down the organizational chart to get things done. We may have role power—the hard power that is granted to us through our official title—but the skills that make up the Interactivity ability are about relational power—the soft power that comes from understanding how to work with people.

In addition to creative and interactive leaders, we will continue to need leaders who can produce. Production in this sense is not about the technical work the leader is completing, but the leader's ability to get work done through others. Future leaders will build future teams capable of executing on the problems the organization has chosen to solve, and they will help their teams grow both personally and professionally. Keeping it all together will also be a challenge requiring future leaders to create a robust system of organization.

THE FUTURE LEADER

Future leaders are those who are effectively and profitably transitioning their organizations from today to tomorrow. Future leaders use the skills of the Future Leadership Framework to help their organizations make this transition. Learning the skills leads to ability. Ability leads to results.

MARATHON

Future leaders must be prepared to play the long game. Going all-in on developing the skills found in the Future Leadership Framework will help you and your organization win the future. But it will require a dedicated and focused long-term effort.

Leadership cannot be done in a sprint. It is always a marathon activity. Leadership, unlike the financial metrics of an organization, shouldn't be measured on a quarterly basis. Leadership success takes time to bloom. It is necessarily a longer process of continuous improvement, not only for the leader, but for the team.

Think about leadership as something to be honed over a

career, not something to be banged out by the end of the year. Leadership is more craftsmanship than injection molding. It is a deliberate process of learning, reflection, and refinement over time.

* * *

YOU HAVE REACHED THE end of the book, but the beginning of your next chapter. By becoming the future leader, you are becoming the leader we all want to have and the leader our organizations need. If you decide to push your chips all-in on these ideas, then continue to Part III of this book for next steps.

Part III

FUTURE LEADER QUICK START GUIDE

20

Future Leader Quick Start Guide

THE FUTURE LEADER QUICK START GUIDE is designed to take the ideas you learned about in the Future Leadership Framework and transform them into actionable tasks. Improving your ability to lead others can only happen with thoughtful and deliberate action.

Since we are all busy, these action steps are spread out over three months—one step each month. Remember, this is a marathon. Take your time. Each step deserves a fair amount of attention.

Ready to get started?

21

Month 1

TAKE THE FUTURE LEADER ASSESSMENT

THE FIRST STEP to making any change is knowing where you are. The following assessment will help you determine how strong your Future Leadership Framework skills and abilities are as of now.

Circle either the "yes" or the "no" for each statement found in the Assessment. "Yes" answers are worth one point. "No" answers are worth zero points. Then, tally your points at the end of each section.

KEEP YOUR BOOK CLEAN!
A free Future Leader Quick Start Guide workbook
(with assessment) is available at
www.FutureLeaderWorkbook.com

FUTURE LEADER ASSESSMENT

CREATIVITY ABILITY

Mission

(Yes / No) I have created a clear, compelling, and actionable mission for the organization.

(Yes / No) I have created a clear, compelling, and actionable mission for my team.

(Yes / No) I frequently revisit my team's mission to assess its ongoing relevance.

(Yes / No) I have created illustrative stories to help communicate the mission.

(Yes / No) My team can tell you what our mission is.

(Yes / No) My team knows why our mission is important.

(Yes / No) Everyone on my team is bought in to our mission.

(Yes / No) I organize all decision making using our mission as the guiding framework.

(Yes / No) I have declined a new initiative because it did not align with our mission.

________ **Mission** Points Subtotal (one point for each "yes")

Synthesis

(Yes / No) My team collects appropriate data regarding the products or services we offer.

(Yes / No) My team regularly creates stories from the data that we collect.

(Yes / No) I often communicate the stories that come from the data.

(Yes / No) My team is comfortable with challenging others' assumptions.

(Yes / No) We regularly get outside opinion on our data and stories.

(Yes / No) I am comfortable when my stories get challenged.

________ **Synthesis** Points Subtotal (one point for each "yes")

Strategy

(Yes / No) Strategic actions over the next three years have been clearly detailed.

(Yes / No) My team's work aligns with our strategies.

(Yes / No) My team is clear on where the organization is in relation to its strategic initiatives.

(Yes / No) We have perspective on long-term strategies and are comfortable with long-term ambiguity.

(Yes / No) I regularly communicate organizational strategies to my team.

(Yes / No) My team understands how their work influences progress on the strategies.

________ **Strategy** Points Subtotal (one point for each "yes")

INTERACTIVITY ABILITY

Relationships

(Yes / No) Most of my relationships are not transactional in nature.

(Yes / No) I feel more than superficially connected to most or all of my team members.

(Yes / No) I know personal details about the members of my team.

(Yes / No) I care about the people I work with.

(Yes / No) I have intentionally built relationships with people across the organization.

(Yes / No) I have intentionally built relationships with other businesses that my organization could team with.

(Yes / No) I regularly create opportunities for others to connect.

(Yes / No) I have intentionally ended at least one business relationship because I considered it "toxic."

________ **Relationships** Points Subtotal (one point for each "yes")

Empathy

(Yes / No) I have taken an emotional intelligence assessment.

(Yes / No) I am not perfect at it, but I express emotions appropriately.

(Yes / No) I regularly attempt to identify emotions in other people.

(Yes / No) Often I adjust my behavior in response to emotions I perceive in others.

(Yes / No) The people I work with sense that I care about them as people.

(Yes / No) I tend to set the example as an emotionally intelligent leader.

________ **Empathy** Points Subtotal (one point for each "yes")

Trust

(Yes / No) My team trusts me.

(Yes / No) I trust my team.

(Yes / No) I often and intentionally align my words with my actions, whether those words or actions are big or small, difficult or easy.

(Yes / No) I intentionally maintain a high level of transparency.

(Yes / No) I regularly communicate big and small information to my team.

(Yes / No) I work to create personal connections with the people in my organization, not just business connections.

________ **Trust** Points Subtotal (one point for each "yes")

PRODUCTIVITY ABILITY

Expectations

(Yes / No) I clearly understand what I want from each of my team members.

(Yes / No) Each member of my team clearly understands what is expected of them.

(Yes / No) I understand, from a broad perspective, where each of my team members are with their work.

(Yes / No) I regularly communicate my expectations to the members of my team.

(Yes / No) I regularly (daily, weekly, or monthly) provide useful feedback to each member of my team.

(Yes / No) I regularly hold members of my team accountable when they miss targets AND when they hit targets.

(Yes / No) I budget time each week to the elements of my program of expectations.

________ **Expectations** Points Subtotal
(one point for each "yes")

Teams

(Yes / No) I have clearly defined what success looks like for my team.

(Yes / No) I regularly communicate what success looks like to my team.

(Yes / No) I have established and communicated performance metrics to my team.

(Yes / No) I actively work to keep my team as small and tight as possible.

(Yes / No) I have built relationships with outside organizations that can be used to supplement my team.

(Yes / No) If my team is distributed, we regularly use technology to maintain human connection (like video conferencing).

(Yes / No) I have fired or reassigned team members who continue to underperform despite my best efforts (at least once).

________ **Teams** Points Subtotal (one point for each "yes")

Training

(Yes / No) My organization has some form of training program already established.

(Yes / No) I take the training and development of my staff seriously.

(Yes / No) Our training programs have been constructed to be more like perks.

(Yes / No) I believe that training should be centered on helping people fulfill their individual potentials in addition to getting better at work tasks.

(Yes / No) I regularly collect feedback about our training programs.

(Yes / No) I have asked others in the organization for their opinion on potential training opportunities.

________ **Training** Points Subtotal (one point for each "yes")

Organization

(Yes / No) I don't hold potential tasks or projects in my head for long before writing them down.

(Yes / No) I tend to record potential tasks or projects in one location.

(Yes / No) I regularly do the initial thinking required to ensure I am clear about what the work actually is.

(Yes / No) I take the time to flesh out projects into constituent tasks.

(Yes / No) I regularly use a calendar for all work and personal appointments, events, birthdays, anniversaries, and more.

(Yes / No) At regular intervals, I purge old stuff from my life.

(Yes / No) I feel comfortable with my level of organization.

________ **Organization** Points Subtotal (one point for each "yes")

CREATIVITY

________ **Mission** Points Subtotal
(from above) - Max of 9

________ **Synthesis** Points Subtotal
(from above) - Max of 6

________ **Strategy** Points Subtotal
(from above) - Max of 6

________ **CREATIVITY ABILITY** Total
(add subtotals together) - Max of 21

INTERACTIVITY

________ **Relationships** Points Subtotal
(from above) - Max of 8

________ **Empathy** Points Subtotal
(from above) - Max of 6

________ **Trust** Points Subtotal
(from above) - Max of 6

________ **INTERACTIVITY ABILITY** Total
(add subtotals together) - Max of 20

PRODUCTIVITY

________ **Expectations** Points Subtotal (from above) - Max of 7

________ **Teams** Points Subtotal (from above) - Max of 7

________ **Training** Points Subtotal (from above) - Max of 6

________ **Organization** Points Subtotal (from above) - Max of 7

________ **PRODUCTIVITY ABILITY** Total (add subtotals together) - Max of 27

FUTURE LEADER ABILITY

________ **TOTAL POINTS** (add Creativity, Interactivity, and Productivity totals) - Max of 68

Future Leader Assessment Key

Based on points, which of the three abilities are you strongest at right now? (Circle one)

Creativity Interactivity Productivity

Based on points, which of the three are you weakest at right now? (Circle one)

Creativity Interactivity Productivity

0-20 Points There is work to do!

What you can do to improve:

1. Read through this book and tune your attention to those areas where you are weakest. Where do you and the ideas diverge?

2. Continue your studies by reading at least one additional book on leadership that focuses on one of the Future Leadership Framework skills.

3. Find a professional coach to help you take your skills to the next level.

4. Encourage your organization to host a Future Leader Workshop. For more information please visit: www.FutureLeaderWorkshop.com.

20 - 50 Points You are making the transition!

What you can do to improve:

1. Encourage your organization to host a Future Leader Workshop. For more information please visit: www.FutureLeaderWorkshop.com.

2. Continue your studies by reading at least one additional book on leadership.

3. Focus on your best skills and double down on developing them further.

4. Identify skills that you need to work on. Where can you make incremental improvements?

50 - 68 Points You are in Future Leader territory! Keep up the good work!

What you can do to stay in topflight condition:

1. At least once each week, block off thirty minutes to reflect solely on your leadership skills. What went well this week? What could be improved upon for next week?

2. Encourage your organization to host a Future Leader Workshop to keep your skills honed. More information at www.FutureLeaderWorkshop.com.

3. Work to identify other potential future leaders and act as a mentor.

4. Find a professional coach to help you take your skills to the next level.

22

Month 2

GET INSANELY ORGANIZED

DURING THE FIRST MONTH, you took the assessment to find out what areas you are strong in and what areas you need to improve. Keep those results in mind as we move into the second month's activity.

Of all the skills in the Future Leadership Framework, the best place to start is with the skill of Organization. Organization, as we saw earlier, is not only about straightening up your desk, files, and to-do lists. It's about creating a comprehensive system that will allow you to effortlessly manage the open loops of your life. Mastering this one skill will permit your mind the freedom and bandwidth to pursue other skills in the framework.

Step 1: Review your current system of organization

(Yes / No) Are you happy with your current system of organization?

How do you tend to keep things organized now? Get detailed on this answer.

What software or physical items do you use to help stay organized?

In your opinion, is this system robust enough to expand into a full system of organization?

Do you completely trust that your calendar has captured every event? (If any mental snag, large or small, came up after you read this, dig into it).

Step 2: Perform a brain dump

With a paper and a pen, start noting everything that comes to mind that you need to track. This includes big tasks, small tasks, little details, work projects, personal projects, actions from others you are waiting on, things you would like to do someday, reminders, one-off thoughts, and more. Write down all things that are pulling at your attention in any way, big or small. I recommend paper and pen because you can do this process faster than typing and it frees you from feeling like you have to sort what you are writing as you write it. No sorting! Not yet anyway. Just let the brain's open loops ooze onto the paper.

Allocate enough time to do this. I recommend holing up in an empty conference room, the public library, a coffee shop, or some other place where you won't be disturbed. Plan on at least two hours. It may take longer. The goal is to allow your brain the time it needs to properly empty its contents. You'll be surprised at how much comes out once you get going.

Step 3: Start sorting what you have written

Now that your mind is free and clear, how do you feel? Take a break from the brain dump before starting to sort what you have written down. Even a day or two is fine if you have other things to tend to.

The next step is to sort what you have written down. Chunking items together by one-off tasks or longer projects is a good way to start. I define a "project" as anything that requires two or more tasks to complete. Even if they are simple tasks, if there are two or more of them, think about it as a project.

Now, look for other ways to sort what you have written down. Maybe you separate the personal from the professional. Maybe you have a group of things you are waiting on from other people. As a pattern-seeing superhero, find the natural fault lines in what you have written and sort accordingly.

Step 4: Transfer the sorted tasks and projects into your system

The right system will effortlessly handle the numerous tasks and projects you are about to enter into it. Lesser systems will falter. Working from lists on legal pads probably won't work for today's leaders who are juggling multiple professional and personal projects. Try software. I use Omnifocus, but there are many others like Trello, Asana, Basecamp, and Evernote.

Step 5: Continually tweak the system as you go

Organization is never done. Your system will need updating on a daily basis. Enter new commitments, and delete tasks and projects that you complete. Understand this to be a living and breathing system and treat it as such. Commit to tweaking the system as you go. It never has to be perfect, it just has to work for you.

Step 6: Go pro with your calendar

If you maintain a clean calendar, then you can skip this step. If your calendar still needs attention, then continue setting up your organizational system with a full calendar update. Here are the calendar action items.

- Add every birthday you know of (spouse, partner, kids, grandkids, parents, friends, aunts, uncles, grandparents, pets, etc.).
- Add every anniversary (work, marriage or dating anniversary, parents, etc.).
- Add every federal holiday and organizational day off.
- Add every vacation (even if they aren't finalized yet).
- Add every kid and partner event (recitals, date nights, etc.).
- Add every personal event regardless of time of day or day of week.
- Add any personal time that you need for thinking or reflection (I recommend at least one thirty-minute block of time per week).
- Review every recurring meeting to determine its continued relevance.
- Review every meeting already planned for the next year.
- Fix any double-booked problems on your calendar, even if it is six months out from today.
- Add any meetings that are still in your head.
- For each event, set a proper interval for recurrence (if needed) and add an appropriate reminder. Reminder notifications might be thirty minutes for a meeting, or three weeks or more for a birthday or anniversary.

- Consider adding travel times for any appointments. If it takes 45 minutes to get to an appointment, considering adding that travel time into the calendar ahead of the event.

Step 7: Purge physical items from your life

With the brain dump done and the tasks, reminders, calendar, and projects somewhat organized, it is time to move into the next phase: clearing out the clutter in your life. This step is about throwing away, recycling, or selling the items that are no longer serving you. If something is no longer serving you, then it should be deleted from your life. You delete it because you want to focus your time and energy on what is serving you.

- Start with your workspace. Go through every file, drawer, and cupboard, and discard what you no longer need. Nothing is off-limits. The purge should include books, files, manuals, receipts, office toys, broken things, reminders, magazines, pens that are out of ink, and broken pencils among other items.
- Are you trying to go paperless? Purchase a high-quality scanner (I have the ScanSnap by Fujitsu) to scan documents before recycling or destroying them.
- Continue the purge at home. Go through every closet, drawer, nook, and room, and get rid of what is no longer serving you. Piles should be divided into charitable donation, the transfer station, and for sale.

- Internalize the notion that the less stuff you have, the less you have to manage, and the less you will have pulling at your attention.

To do this well may take some time depending on how much stuff you have collected.

Step 8: Maintain vigilance

A system of organization is something that you will have to tend to for the rest of your life. Entropy is the natural process for all things. Your system will also break down if you don't spend time on it. Regularly schedule time to update and tweak your system of organization and to purge the things that are no longer serving you. Putting this on your calendar as a recurring event will help you succeed. I find that the time around the first of a year is a good time for this project. Remember the overall goal: You want a clear head so that you can be fully present for the work that we desperately need you to do.

* * *

MOST OF THESE ITEMS can be completed in one month with dedicated focus. If you find it takes longer than a month, then that is perfectly fine. Continue the process until the work is done.

23

Month 3

RENEW THE MISSION

If you are responsible for the mission of the entire organization, then you will need time to focus on that mission. If you are responsible for a team within the organization, then this is the time to create or tweak the team's mission. Each organization should have a clear, compelling, and actionable mission and each team within an organization should have a clear, compelling, and actionable mission that supports the overall mission.

Missions serve as the foundation that everything else gets built on top of. Spend month three on mission and then evaluate how the clarity affects your team.

Step 1: Review the current mission

(Yes / No) Does your organization have a clear, compelling, and actionable mission?

If yes, then consider yourself lucky!

If no, then depending on your position, you may have to do your best to define the organization's mission so that you can create a team mission that aligns.

(Yes / No) Does your team have a clear, compelling, and actionable mission?

If yes, then you rock!

If no, then there is some work to do with your team to get the mission created.

(Yes / No) Do your team's actions actually align with its mission?

If yes, then you are way ahead of the game. Take some time to review your strategies and key performance indicators to ensure everything is still in alignment.

If no, then this is where matching actions with words gets real. The whole point of a mission is to be a framework to help guide decision-making. Once you create your team's mission, then creating strategies and key performance indicators that align with that mission comes next.

(Yes / No) Have any metrics (key performance indicators) been established to measure success against the mission?

If yes, awesome!

If no, then consider the following cascade: beliefs flow to vision, which flows to mission, which flows to strategies, which flows to key performance indicators (KPIs). KPIs are the metrics your team will use to gauge success against their mission. KPIs are further broken down into actions that support each KPI. These are the actions your team should be spending their time working on.

Step 2: Check for understanding and comprehension

Ask yourself and each member of your team, "How would you describe our mission?"

Considering the information above, ask yourself and each member of your team, "How do you know we are making progress toward that mission?"

Asking these kinds of questions may elicit curiosity from your team members. Be upfront and explain why you are asking and what you are looking to do. The best answers will be candid. Create an environment that permits these candid responses (this goes back to the Future Leadership Framework skill of Trust).

Step 3: Think through the process of creating or renewing the mission

The questions below can help guide you.

Who should be involved in the process of renewing the mission?

What does the process of renewing the mission look like (weekly meetings, email, drafting, virtual meetings, etc.)?

When would you like to have the work done?

Who (if anyone) has to know about or approve what you are doing?

What does success look like when it comes to renewing the mission?

Step 4: Reset expectations

Once all of the thinking behind the initiative has been completed, it's time to proceed with the work. First, reset the expectations with your team. Hold an all-hands meeting to discuss the process and importance of renewing the mission.

Step 5: Begin the work on the mission

You have identified who will help on the project and how the process should unfold. You have created a timeline for the work and have reset your team's expectations. The following tips can help as you continue momentum.

TIP 1: Sequester your team. Conference rooms work fine. It would be better to have people meet off-site, such as a restaurant or library meeting room.

TIP 2: Missions don't need to be grand. The simpler, the better. As you are drafting, boil the words down to the basics. Use plain English, and keep it as short as possible.

TIP 3: Use a whiteboard, or an easel-sized writing pad. Better are the jumbo sticky notes that can be stuck on the wall as you work and taken with you when you leave. Bring markers, pens, and legal pads as well.

TIP 4: Fall in love with the drafting process. There are no dumb ideas and no dumb comments. Capture everything. You want every idea. Set the expectation from the beginning that all ideas, no matter how scattered, are welcome.

TIP 5: Expect to rework the material a number of times. This is part of the drafting process.

Step 6: Get outside opinion on later drafts

Don't be afraid to get outside opinion on the mission. Run it by other people and get their impression and their feedback. This is helpful during the overall drafting process.

Step 7: Finalize your mission

Self-explanatory. Finalize the organization's or the team's mission!

Step 8: Communicate it widely

Print it up. Put it onto the back of business cards. Put it on wallet cards. Create stories that help to illustrate the mission. Talk often about the mission and its importance.

* * *

AS YOU CAN SEE FROM the steps above, this is a process that will require your time and attention to get right. Expect that urgent daily work will always compete for your attention. Think of a mission as the fundamental motivational and clarity-creating vehicle that it is. Without a clear, compelling, and actionable mission, your work, and your team's work, will always lack context.

24

Future Months

CREATE A SUCCESS PLAN

SUCCESS IS NOT AUTOMATIC. It requires planning and attention. Becoming the future leader requires the same.

At this point you have completed the Future Leader Assessment, created a system of organization designed to manage the various moving parts of your life, and renewed your team's mission. You have the foundation on which to build the superstructure of success. How should you continue to move forward in the months and years to come?

Consider the steps as outlined below.

Future Leader Success Plan

Create Personal Appointment Blocks

Add a recurring half-hour weekly appointment block to your calendar dedicated only to thinking, reflection, and personal progress. This is where thoughts get turned into future actions, so make these sessions a priority.

From your Future Leader Assessment, rank your scores for each skill, from highest to lowest.

Highest

1. ______________________
2. ______________________
3. ______________________
4. ______________________
5. ______________________
6. ______________________
7. ______________________
8. ______________________
9. ______________________
10. ______________________

Lowest

Starting with the skill you are best at, and during some portion of the half-hour appointment block you have each week, reread the portion of the chapter on ideas for implementation.

Reflect on how you can increase your competence in that skill. Write down your reflections. How can your ideas be implemented in small actions?

Turn your reflections into one or two small actions to take over the next week. The goal is not quantity, but systematic improvement.

During future appointment blocks, continue to work on the skills as listed above. If a week is too short of an interval, then change the interval to whatever best serves you.

Consult Other Resources

Go onto Amazon.com or BarnesAndNoble.com and look for one book that could help you improve one of your top three strongest skills.

Encourage your organization to host a Future Leader Workshop. Go to www.FutureLeaderWorkshop.com for more details.

Hire a professional coach to help you break through learning and performance plateaus. The International Coach Federation is the industry association for professional coaches. More can be found at www.CoachFederation.org.

Consider having a 360-degree review done. These performance

reviews seek the input from your colleagues, people you lead, and your superiors for insights into your leadership style.

Making the transition to a future leader may happen quickly, or not. But, in this case, the journey is more important than the destination.

* * *

I AM CONFIDENT, as you should be, that the tools and implementation plans presented in this book will help you and your organization win the future. But none of this works unless you do. Commit to the process, evaluate what is working and what is not working, make changes, and focus on becoming the type of leader that we desperately need.

If I may assist you in any way, or if you would like to get in touch on any other matter, please send me an email at:

Jonathan@SandcastleCompany.com

I wish you continued success!

About the Author

JONATHAN WILSON writes, speaks, and consults on the future of leadership. He is the owner of Sandcastle Company, a Seattle-based leadership consulting organization. Jonathan works with organizations on leadership issues and helps experienced leaders reboot their leadership style to succeed in a workplace that is being radically reshaped by the changing generations and advancing technology. Additionally, Jonathan is a keynote speaker on the future of leadership. Jonathan has a master's degree in public administration from Seattle University and professional-coach training from the University of Miami. Jonathan has held leadership and management positions in both the public and private sectors for many years. When not working he enjoys wrestling with his elementary-aged kids, playing the ukulele, and sitting on distant sunny beaches (especially when it's raining in Seattle).

Say hi...

on Twitter @jonathanwilson1
on Linkedin @jonathanwilson2010
on email Jonathan@SandcastleCompany.com

How can I help your organization win the future?

Taking the Future Leadership Framework Beyond the Page

FUTURE LEADER KEYNOTE PRESENTATION

Turning everyday leaders into future leaders is key for any organization looking to thrive, especially over the next ten years. The workplace is experiencing a radical change as it starts to permanently bend in response to the forces of generational churn and rapid technological advancement. The days of management by spreadsheets are over. We need authentic and effective leadership that is tuned to the times now more than ever before. In this engaging, inspiring, and dynamic keynote presentation, Jonathan will help transition your leaders into future leaders. Using a combination of science, case studies, stories, and humor, Jonathan will provide your team the actionable takeaways they need to start leading more effectively the very next day.

Get more information about having Jonathan speak at your event by visiting: **www.FutureLeaderSpeaker.com**

FUTURE LEADER WORKSHOP

A number of us start off as technicians—the people who do the hands-on work—in our organizations. One day we accept a promotion that requires us to transform from technicians into leaders. We go from managing just ourselves and our work to being responsible for moving others to action. The problem is that while we might have trained for years to become a great technician, many of us haven't yet put that same level of effort into being a great leader. The Future Leader Workshop can help. These one-day workshops deep dive on the concepts and actions of the Future Leadership Framework to help attendees become leaders that get remarkable results. Each attendee will not only learn the Future Leadership Framework skills, but they will also leave with customized and actionable takeaways that will help them implement those skills right away.

Get more information about having Jonathan work with your organization by visiting: **www.FutureLeaderWorkshop.com**

Special Thanks

SPECIAL THANKS GO TO my family for listening to and challenging my ideas, and for putting up with my writing schedule. Billie, Arabella, and Cooper—thank you for supporting me on this journey!

Special thanks also goes to my Book Launch Team. Each has provided unique guidance and assistance during the final push to get this book from draft to final. Some helped by reading sections and making comments, others by encouraging me to keep making progress on this marathon project. Thank you!

The Book Launch Team members include: Ben Wilson, Bob Givnin, Carl Hung, Carmen Ludtke, Christina Delia, Cory Schutz, Desiree Perez, Diana De La Torriente, Eric Mercado, Gordon Alvord, James Looper, Jennifer Donohue, Jessica Dowches-Wheeler, Jim Williams, Kevin Kato, Lindsey Nickell, Lynn Uppinghouse, Melissa Stack, Michelle Givnin, Rich Mueller, Sandy Wilson, Seida Wood, Serena Brancacio, Shari Matz, Sue Wallace, Teresa Bravo, and Terry Carter.

Notes

Chapter 1: The Clarion Call for the Future Leader

1. No sources cited.

Chapter 2: Leadership on the Rocks

1. Scott Reckard, "Wells Fargo's Pressure-Cooker Sales Culture Comes at a Cost," *Los Angeles Times*, December 21, 2013, http://www.latimes.com/business/la-fi-wells-fargo-sale-pressure-20131222-story.html.
2. "Wells Fargo Today," Wells Fargo, accessed February 3, 2018, www.wellsfargo.com/assets/pdf/about/corporate/wells-faro-today.pdf.
3. Hearing on an Examination of Wells Fargo's Unauthorized Accounts and the Regulatory Response, September 20, 2016, page 75; Committee on Banking, Housing, and Urban Affairs; 114th Congress; Records of the United States Senate.
4. Hearing on an Examination of Wells Fargo's Unauthorized Accounts and the Regulatory Response, September 20, 2016, page 75; Committee on Banking, Housing, and Urban Affairs; 114th Congress; Records of the United States Senate.
5. Hearing on an Examination of Wells Fargo's Unauthorized Accounts and the Regulatory Response, September 20, 2016, page 75; Committee on Banking, Housing, and Urban Affairs; 114th Congress; Records of the United States Senate.

6. Scott Reckard, "Wells Fargo's Pressure-Cooker Sales Culture Comes at a Cost," *Los Angeles Times*, December 21, 2013, http://www.latimes.com/business/la-fi-wells-fargo-sale-pressure-20131222-story.html.
7. Bill Chappell, "Wells Fargo Fined $185 Million Over Creation of Fake Accounts for Bonuses," *NPR*, September 8, 2016, https://www.npr.org/sections/thetwo-way/2016/09/08/493130449/wells-fargo-to-pay-around-190-million-over-fake-accounts-that-sparked-bonuses.
8. Matt Egan, "Wells Fargo Victims get Closer to Payback in $142 Million Settlement," *CNNMoney*, July 10, 2017, http://money.cnn.com/2017/07/10/investing/wells-fargo-fake-account-settlement/index.html?iid=EL.
9. Russell Hotten, "Volkswagen: The Scandal Explained," *BBC*, December 10, 2015, http://www.bbc.com/news/business-34324772.
10. Russell Hotten, "Volkswagen: The Scandal Explained," *BBC*, December 10, 2015, http://www.bbc.com/news/business-34324772.
11. "Frequently Asked Questions," Small Business Administration, accessed on February 3, 2018, https://www.sba.gov/sites/default/files/FAQ_Sept_2012.pdf.
12. "Frequently Asked Questions," Small Business Administration, accessed on February 3, 2018, https://www.sba.gov/sites/default/files/FAQ_Sept_2012.pdf.
13. "Frequently Asked Questions," Small Business Administration, accessed on February 3, 2018, https://www.sba.gov/sites/default/files/FAQ_Sept_2012.pdf.
14. Annamarie Mann and Jim Harter, "The Worldwide Employee Engagement Crisis," *Gallup*, January 7, 2016, http://news.gallup.com/businessjournal/188033/worldwide-employee-engagement-crisis.aspx.
15. Annamarie Mann and Jim Harter, "The Worldwide Employee Engagement Crisis," *Gallup*, January 7, 2016, http://news.gallup.com/businessjournal/188033/worldwide-employee-engagement-crisis.aspx.
16. "2016 Udemy Workplace Boredom Study," Udemy, 2016, accessed on August 24, 2017, https://info.udemy.com/rs/273-CKQ-053/images2016_Udemy_Workplace_Boredom_Study.pdf?_ga=2.169774113.1680810006.1503069830-2055964198.1503069830.

17. "2016 Udemy Workplace Boredom Study," Udemy, 2016, accessed on August 24, 2017, https://info.udemy.com/rs/273-CKQ-053/images2016_Udemy_Workplace_Boredom_Study.pdf?_ga=2.169774113.1680810006.1503069830-2055964198.1503069830.

18. Jim Harter, "Obsolete Annual Reviews: Gallup's Advice," *Gallup*, September 28, 2015, http://www.gallup.com/opinion/gallup/185921/obsolete-annual-reviews-gallup-advice.aspx.

19. Jim Harter, "Obsolete Annual Reviews: Gallup's Advice," *Gallup*, September 28, 2015, http://www.gallup.com/opinion/gallup/185921/obsolete-annual-reviews-gallup-advice.aspx.

20. Jacob Shriar, "Employee Feedback: The Complete Guide," *OfficeVibe*, https://www.officevibe.com/employee-engagement-solution/employee-feedback.

21. Jacob Shriar, "Employee Feedback: The Complete Guide," *OfficeVibe*, https://www.officevibe.com/employee-engagement-solution/employee-feedback.

22. Jacob Shriar, "Employee Feedback: The Complete Guide," *OfficeVibe*, https://www.officevibe.com/employee-engagement-solution/employee-feedback.

23. Amelia Peacock, "Engage Millennial Employees with Feedback and Evaluation," *Clutch*, December 7, 2016, https://clutch.co/hr/resources/engage-millennial-employees-feedback-evaluation.

24. Amelia Peacock, "Engage Millennial Employees with Feedback and Evaluation," *Clutch*, December 7, 2016, https://clutch.co/hr/resources/engage-millennial-employees-feedback-evaluation.

25. Amelia Peacock, "Engage Millennial Employees with Feedback and Evaluation," *Clutch*, December 7, 2016, https://clutch.co/hr/resources/engage-millennial-employees-feedback-evaluation.

26. "How Millennials Want to Work and Live," Gallup, accessed on December 6, 2017, http://news.gallup.com/reports/189830/e.aspx#aspnetForm.

27. "Many Employees in North America and the United Kingdom Are Not Happy at Work, According to Achievers' Latest Study," Achievers, September 9, 2015, https://www.achievers.com/press/many-employees-north-america-and-united-kingdom-are-not-happy-work-according-achievers-latest/.

28. Timothy Devinney, "All Talk, No Action: Why Company Strategy Often Falls on Deaf Ears," *The Conversation*, March 25, 2013, https://theconversation.com/all-talk-no-action-why-company-strategy-often-falls-on-deaf-ears-12788.

29. Timothy Devinney, "All Talk, No Action: Why Company Strategy Often Falls on Deaf Ears," *The Conversation*, March 25, 2013, https://theconversation.com/all-talk-no-action-why-company-strategy-often-falls-on-deaf-ears-12788.

30. Chris McChesney, Sean Covey, Jim Huling, *The 4 Disciplines of Execution* (New York: Free Press, 2012), 5.

31. "Trust in Employee Engagement: Data Reveals Employee Trust Divide," Edelman, accessed on August 19, 2017, http://www.edelman.com/insights/intellectual-property/2016-edelman-trust-barometer/state-of-trust/employee-trust-divide/.

32. "Trust in Employee Engagement: Data Reveals Employee Trust Divide," Edelman, accessed on August 19, 2017, http://www.edelman.com/insights/intellectual-property/2016-edelman-trust-barometer/state-of-trust/employee-trust-divide/.

33. "Global Generations 3.0: A Global Study on Trust in the Workplace," EY, accessed on February 3, 2018, http://www.ey.com/Publication/vwLUAssets/ey-could-trust-cost-you-a-generation-of-talent/$FILE/ey-could-trust-cost-you-a-generation-of-talent.pdf.

34. From the Kronos website, https://www.kronos.com/about-us.

35. "The Employee Burnout Crisis: Study Reveals Big Workplace Challenge In 2017," Kronos, January 9, 2017, https://www.kronos.com/about-us/newsroom/employee-burnout-crisis-study-reveals-big-workplace-challenge-2017.

36. "The Employee Burnout Crisis: Study Reveals Big Workplace Challenge In 2017," Kronos, January 9, 2017, https://www.kronos.com/about-us/newsroom/employee-burnout-crisis-study-reveals-big-workplace-challenge-2017.

37. Eric Garton, "Employee Burnout Is a Problem with the Company Not the Person," *Harvard Business Review*, April 6, 2017, https://hbr.org/2017/04/employee-burnout-is-a-problem-with-the-company-not-the-person.

38. "The State of American Vacation 2017," Project: Time Off, accessed on December 7, 2017, https://www.projecttimeoff.com/sites/default/files/StateofAmericanVacation2017.pdf.

39. "The State of American Vacation 2017," Project: Time Off, accessed on December 7, 2017, https://www.projecttimeoff.com/sites/default/files/StateofAmericanVacation2017.pdf.

40. "The State of American Vacation 2017," Project: Time Off, accessed on December 7, 2017, https://www.projecttimeoff.com/sites/default/files/StateofAmericanVacation2017.pdf.

41. "The State of American Vacation 2017," Project: Time Off, accessed on December 7, 2017, https://www.projecttimeoff.com/sites/default/files/StateofAmericanVacation2017.pdf.

42. Shawn Achor, "Do Vacations Make Us Happier? The Answer: It Depends," *Huffington Post*, March 26, 2014, https://www.huffingtonpost.com/shawn-achor/do-vacations-make-us-happ_b_5022511.html.

43. Susan Sorenson, "How Employee Engagement Drives Growth," *Gallup*, June 20, 2013, http://www.gallup.com/businessjournal/163130/employee-engagement-drives-growth.aspx.

44. Susan Sorenson, "How Employee Engagement Drives Growth," *Gallup*, June 20, 2013, http://www.gallup.com/businessjournal/163130/employee-engagement-drives-growth.aspx.

45. If we take $550,000,000 which is the cost of actively disengaged employees and divide it by the 125,967,000 total people 16 years old or older that are in the labor force we get $4,366.22 (https://www.bls.gov/cps/cpsaat08.htm).

46. "The High Cost of Doing Nothing: Quantifying the Impact of Leadership on the Bottom Line," Ken Blanchard Companies, 2009, http://www.blanchard-bg.com/Materials/Blanchard_The_High_Cost_of_Doing_Nothing.pdf.

47. Jim Harter and Amy Adkins, "Employees Want A Lot More From Their Managers," *Gallup*, April 8, 2015, http://www.gallup.com/businessjournal/182321/employees-lot-managers.aspx.

48. "2016 Human Capital Benchmarking Report," Society for Human Resource Management, November 2016, https://www.shrm.org/hr-today/trends-and-forecasting/research-and-surveys/Documents/2016-Human-Capital-Report.pdf.

49. Heather Boushey and Sarah Jane Glynn, "There are Significant Business Costs to Replacing Employees," *The Center for American Progress*, November 6, 2012, https://www.americanprogress.org/issues/economy/reports/2012/11/16/44464/there-are-significant-business-costs-to-replacing-employees/.

50. Heather Boushey and Sarah Jane Glynn, "There are Significant Business Costs to Replacing Employees," *The Center for American Progress*, November 6, 2012, https://www.americanprogress.org/issues/economy/reports/2012/11/16/44464/there-are-significant-business-costs-to-replacing-employees/.

Chapter 3: The Force of Generational Churn

1. Mark P. Mattson, "Superior Pattern Processing is the Essence of the Evolved Human Brain," *Frontiers in Neuroscience*, (August 2014): 265. Found online at https://www.ncbi.nlm.nih.gov/pmc/articles/PMC4141622/.

2. Mark P. Mattson, "Superior Pattern Processing is the Essence of the Evolved Human Brain," *Frontiers in Neuroscience*, (August 2014): 265. Found online at https://www.ncbi.nlm.nih.gov/pmc/articles/PMC4141622/.

3. Michael Shermer, "Patternicity: Finding Meaningful Patterns in Meaningless Noise," *Scientific American*, December 1, 2008, https://www.scientificamerican.com/article/patternicity-finding-meaningful-patterns/.

4. Karen Workman, "The Challenger Space Shuttle Disaster, 30 Years Later," *The New York Times*, January 26, 2016, https://www.nytimes.com/interactive/2016/01/29/science/space/challenger-explosion-30-year-anniversary.html.

5. Karl Mannheim, "Problem of Generations," in the *Essays on the Sociology of Knowledge*, ed. Paul Kecskemeti (London: Routledge and Kegan Paul), 276-320. Found online at http://www.history.ucsb.edu/faculty/marcuse/classes/201/articles/27MannheimGenerations.pdf.

6. Richard Fry, "Millennials Surpass Gen Xers as Largest Generation in the US Labor Force," *Pew Research Center*, May 11, 2015, http://www.pewresearch.org/fact-tank/2015/05/11/millennials-surpass-gen-xers-as-the-largest-generation-in-u-s-labor-force/.

7. Karl Mannheim, "Problem of Generations," in the *Essays on the Sociology of Knowledge*, ed. Paul Kecskemeti (London: Routledge and Kegan Paul), 276-320. Found online at http://www.history.ucsb.edu/faculty/marcuse/classes/201/articles/27MannheimGenerations.pdf.
8. Karl Mannheim, "Problem Of Generations," in the *Essays on the Sociology of Knowledge*, ed. Paul Kecskemeti (London: Routledge and Kegan Paul), 276-320. Found online at http://www.history.ucsb.edu/faculty/marcuse/classes/201/articles/27MannheimGenerations.pdf.
9. Internet usage around the world from Internet World Stats found at http://www.internetworldstats.com/stats.htm, accessed on July 31, 2017.
10. D'Vera Cohn and Paul Taylor, "Baby Boomers Approach 65 - Glumly," *Pew Research Center*, December 20, 2010, http://www.pewsocial-trends.org/2010/12/20/baby-boomers-approach-65-glumly/.
11. Information found via an interactive map at Aperion Care at https://aperioncare.com/blog/retirement-age-around-world/, accessed on February 8, 2018.
12. Employee tenure information found in an Economic News Release dated September 22, 2016, from the Bureau of Labor Statistics, https://www.bls.gov/news.release/tenure.nr0.htm, accessed on February 8, 2018.
13. Dan Schawbel, "Millennials vs. Baby Boomers: Who Would You Rather Hire?" *Time*, March 29, 2012, http://business.time.com/2012/03/29/millennials-vs-baby-boomers-who-would-you-rather-hire/.
14. Lindsey Pollak, "In 5 Years, Millennials Will Make Up 50% Of The Workforce," *ThinkAdvisor*, January 7, 2015, http://www.thinkadvisor.com/2015/01/07/in-5-years-millennials-will-make-up-50-of-the-work.
15. Morley Winograd and Michael Hais, "How Millennials Could Upend Wall Street and Corporate America," *Brookings*, May 2014, https://www.brookings.edu/wp-content/uploads/2016/06/Brookings_Winogradfinal.pdf.
16. Employee tenure information found in an Economic News Release dated September 22, 2016, from the Bureau of Labor Statistics, https://www.bls.gov/news.release/tenure.nr0.htm, accessed on February 8, 2018.

17. "Millennials at Work: Reshaping the Workplace," PwC, 2011, https://www.pwc.com/m1/en/services/consulting/documents/millennials-at-work.pdf.

18. "Millennials at Work: Reshaping the Workplace," PwC, 2011, https://www.pwc.com/m1/en/services/consulting/documents/millennials-at-work.pdf.

Chapter 4: The Force of Rapid Technological Advancement

1. "The Story of the Intel 4004," Intel, accessed on February 16, 2018, https://www.intel.com/content/www/us/en/history/museum-story-of-intel-4004.html.

2. "The Story of the Intel 4004," Intel, accessed on February 16, 2018, https://www.intel.com/content/www/us/en/history/museum-story-of-intel-4004.html.

3. Gordon Moore, "Cramming More Components onto Integrated Circuits," *Electronics*, April 19, 1965, https://www.cs.utexas.edu/~fussell/courses/cs352h/papers/moore.pdf.

4. John Brockman, "Stuart Kauffman—The Adjacent Possible," *Edge*, November 9, 2003, https://www.edge.org/conversation/stuart_a_kauffman-the-adjacent-possible.

5. Oliver Burkeman, "Steven Johnson: 'Eureka Moments are Very, Very Rare,'" *The Guardian*, October 19, 2010, https://www.theguardian.com/science/2010/oct/19/steven-johnson-good-ideas.

6. "Wright Brothers First Flight," National Park Service, April 14, 2015, https://www.nps.gov/wrbr/learn/historyculture/thefirstflight.htm.

7. "The Early Years of Air Transportation: 1914-1927," Smithsonian National Air and Space Museum, accessed on June 24, 2017, https://airandspace.si.edu/exhibitions/america-by-air/online/early_years/early_years01.cfm.

8. "Timeline of FAA and Aerospace History," The Federal Aviation Administration, accessed on December 20, 2017, https://www.faa.gov/about/history/timeline/.

9. "Timeline of FAA and Aerospace History," The Federal Aviation Administration, accessed on December 20, 2017, https://www.faa.gov/about/history/timeline/.

10. "The 707/720 Commercial Transport," The Boeing Company, accessed on December 20, 2017, http://www.boeing.com/history/products/707.page.

11. Labor force statistics are found in the current population survey produced by the Bureau of Labor Statistics. The chart can be found here: https://data.bls.gov/timeseries/LNS12000000 (accessed on February 16, 2018).

12. "Employment, Hours, and Earnings from the Current Employment Statistics Survey," Bureau of Labor Statistics, accessed on February 16, 2018, https://data.bls.gov/timeseries/CES3000000001.

13. "Industrial Production: Manufacturing," St. Louis Fed, accessed on July 9, 2018, https://fred.stlouisfed.org/series/IPMANSICS.

14. Patrick Gillespie, "Rise of the Machines: Fear Robots, Not China or Mexico," *CNN Money*, January 30, 2017, http://money.cnn.com/2017/01/30/news/economy/jobs-china-mexico-automation/?iid=EL.

15. Wolfgang Lehmacher, "Don't Blame China for Taking U.S. Jobs," *Fortune*, November 8, 2016, http://fortune.com/2016/11/08/china-automation-jobs/.

16. Michael J. Hicks and Srikant Devaraj, "The Myth and Reality of Manufacturing in America," *Ball State University*, June 2013, https://projects.cberdata.org/reports/MfgReality.pdf.

17. Harold L. Sirkin, Michael Zinser, and Justin Rose, "The Robotics Revolution: The Next Great Leap in Manufacturing," *Boston Consulting Group*. September 23, 2015, https://www.bcgperspectives.com/content/articles/lean-manufacturing-innovation-robotics-revolution-next-great-leap-manufacturing/.

18. Michael Chui, James Manyika, and Mehdi Miremadi, "Where Machines Can Replace Humans, And Where They Can't (Yet)," *McKinsey Quarterly*, July 2016, https://www.mckinsey.com/business-functions/digital-mckinsey/our-insights/where-machines-could-replace-humans-and-where-they-cant-yet.

19. Information about Kira Systems found on their website, https://kirasystems.com/, accessed on December 20, 2017.

20. Steve Lohr, "A.I. Is Doing Legal Work. But It Won't Replace Lawyers, Yet," *The New York Times*, March 19, 2017, https://www.nytimes.com/2017/03/19/technology/lawyers-artificial-intelligence.html.

21. "Terminal 4, Changi International Airport," Airport Technology, accessed on February 16, 2018, http://www.airport-technology.com/projects/terminal-4-changi-international-airport-singapore/.
22. Ray Kurzweil, *The Singularity Is Near* (New York: Penguin Books, 2006), page 50.
23. Ray Kurzweil, *The Singularity Is Near* (New York: Penguin Books, 2006), page 50.
24. Ben Hammersley, "Live in London," podcast interview with Natalie Campbell, Future Visions, December 5, 2017, audio, 07:39, https://itunes.apple.com/us/podcast/future-visions/id1259298623?mt=2.
25. Salena Zito, "Here's Another Industry Amazon Is Killing Off," *New York Post*, February 10, 2018, https://nypost.com/2018/02/10/heres-another-industry-amazon-is-killing-off/?utm_campaign=iosapp&utm_source=mail_app.
26. "Costco Code of Ethics," Costco, accessed on February 16, 2018, https://www.costco.ca/about-us.html.
27. "Costco Code of Ethics," Costco, accessed on February 16, 2018, https://www.costco.ca/about-us.html.

Chapter 5: Win the Future

1. No sources cited.

Chapter 6: CREATIVITY

1. Definition found at Dictionary.com, http://www.dictionary.com/browse/creativity, accessed on May 31, 2018.

Chapter 7: Mission: Find the Right Problems to Solve

1. Steve Garber, "Sputnik and the Dawn of the Space Age," *NASA*, October 10, 2007, https://history.nasa.gov/sputnik/.
2. "May 25, 1961: JFK's Moon shot Speech to Congress," SPACE.com, May 25, 2011, https://www.space.com/11772-president-kennedy-historic-speech-moon-space.html.

3. "Apollo 11 Mission Overview," NASA, accessed on February 18, 2018, https://www.nasa.gov/mission_pages/apollo/missions/apollo11.html.
4. ASOS mission statement found at https://www.asosplc.com. Accessed on February 18, 2018.
5. TED mission statement found at https://www.ted.com/about/our-organization. Accessed on September 1, 2017.
6. Information about SpaceX found at http://www.spacex.com/about. Accessed on August 31, 2017.
7. Information about SpaceX found at http://www.spacex.com/about. Accessed on August 31, 2017.
8. Refer back to Chapter 2 for this statistic.
9. Sonny Chheng and Alyson Daichendt, "Mission, Meaning, And The Millennials," *Deloitte*, April 6, 2017, https://hrtimesblog.com/2017/04/06/mission-meaning-and-millennials/.
10. Brandon Rigoni and Bailey Nelson, "Millennials Not Connecting With Their Company's Mission," *Gallup*, November 15, 2016, http://www.gallup.com/businessjournal/167633/why-company-mission-driven.aspx.

Chapter 8: Synthesis: Create Stories from Data

1. Information from the Real Time Statistics Project can be found at https://realtimestatistics.org/projects.php. Internet statistics can be found at http://www.internetlivestats.com. Both were accessed on September 25, 2017.
2. "The Digital Universe of Opportunities: Rich Data and the Increasing Value of the Internet of Things," EMC, April 2014, https://www.emc.com/leadership/digital-universe/2014iview/executive-summary.htm.
3. Tom Popomoronis, "Prime Day Gives Amazon Over 600 Reasons Per Second to Celebrate," *Inc.*, July 13, 2016, https://www.inc.com/tom-popomaronis/amazon-just-eclipsed-records-selling-over-600-items-per-second.html.
4. Lauren Thomas, "Amazon Prime Day Breaks Record; Sales Grew by More Than 60 Percent," *CNBC*, July 12, 2017, https://www.cnbc.com/2017/07/12/amazon-prime-day-breaks-record-event-grew-by-more-than-60-percent.html.

5. Teena Maddox, "Research: 30 Percent of Organizations Collecting Big Data," *ZDNet*, March 2, 2015, http://www.zdnet.com/article/research-30-percent-of-organizations-collecting-big-data/.
6. "A Guide to the Internet of Things Infographic," Intel, accessed on February 19, 2018, https://www.intel.com/content/www/us/en/internet-of-things/infographics/guide-to-iot.html.
7. Adi Gaskell, "Becoming A Data Driven Organization," *Forbes*, October 28, 2016, https://www.forbes.com/sites/adigaskell/2016/10/28/becoming-a-data-driven-organization/#3f896f564121.
8. Phil Ryan, "Millennials Have Least Analytical Acumen, AMA Study Suggests," *American Management Association*, accessed on February 19, 2018, http://www.amanet.org/training/articles/millennials-have-least-analytical-acumen-ama-study-suggests.aspx.
9. Mikhail Zinshteyn, "The Skills Gap: America's Young Workers Are Lagging Behind," *The Atlantic*, February 17, 2015, https://www.theatlantic.com/education/archive/2015/02/the-skills-gap-americas-young-workers-are-lagging-behind/385560/.
10. Stuart Wolpert, "Is Technology Producing A Decline in Critical Thinking And Analysis?" *UCLA*, January 27, 2009, http://newsroom.ucla.edu/releases/is-technology-producing-a-decline-79127.
11. Randy Bean, "How Big Data Is Empowering AI and Machine Learning at Scale," *MIT Sloan Review*, May 8, 2017, http://sloanreview.mit.edu/article/how-big-data-is-empowering-ai-and-machine-learning-at-scale/.
12. Information about Watson found at https://www.ibm.com/watson/stories/. Accessed on September 30, 2017.

Chapter 9: Strategy: Set the Organization's Sail

1. Jim Romenesko, "Starbucks Chairman Warns of 'The Commoditization of the Starbucks Experience,'" *Starbucks Gossip*, February 23, 2007, http://starbucksgossip.typepad.com/_/2007/02/starbucks_chair_2.html.

2. Jim Romenesko, "Starbucks Chairman Warns of 'The Commoditization of the Starbucks Experience,'" *Starbucks Gossip*, February 23, 2007, http://starbucksgossip.typepad.com/_/2007/02/starbucks_chair_2.html.
3. Howard Schultz, "Live Episode! Starbucks: Howard Schultz," interview by Guy Raz, *How I Built This*, September 27, 2017, audio, http://one.npr.org/?sharedMediaId=551874532:554086519.
4. Stock price is $56.10 as of February 22, 2018. Information about store counts found on the Starbucks site at https://www.starbucks.com/about-us/company-information/starbucks-company-timeline.
5. Howard Schultz, "Live Episode! Starbucks: Howard Schultz," interview by Guy Raz, *How I Built This*, September 27, 2017, audio, http://one.npr.org/?sharedMediaId=551874532:554086519.
6. Information about store counts found on the Starbucks site at https://www.starbucks.com/about-us/company-information/starbucks-company-timeline. Accessed on February 22, 2018.
7. Information about store counts found on the Starbucks site at https://www.starbucks.com/about-us/company-information/starbucks-company-timeline. Accessed on February 22, 2018.
8. "MEDIA ALERT: Starbucks Closes Between 5:30 and 9:00 P.M. on Tuesday to Perfect the Art of Espresso," Starbucks Press Release, February 24, 2008, https://news.starbucks.com/news/media-alert-starbucks-closes-between-530-and-900-p.m.-on-tuesday-to-perfect.
9. Melissa Allison, "Starbucks stores to shut 3 hours on Feb 26 for retraining baristas," *The Seattle Times*, February 12, 2008, https://www.seattletimes.com/business/starbucks-stores-to-shut-3-hours-on-feb-26-for-retraining-baristas/.
10. Melissa Allison, "Starbucks stores to shut 3 hours on Feb 26 for retraining baristas," *The Seattle Times*, February 12, 2008, https://www.seattletimes.com/business/starbucks-stores-to-shut-3-hours-on-feb-26-for-retraining-baristas/.
11. No Author Located, "Coffee Break for Starbucks 135,000 Baristas," *CNN Money*, February 26, 2008, http://money.cnn.com/2008/02/25/news/companies/starbucks/index.htm.

12. Howard Schultz, "Howard Schultz Transformation Agenda Communication #3," *Starbucks Newsroom*, January 29, 2008, https://news.starbucks.com/news/howard-schultz-transformation-agenda-communication-3.

13. Howard Schultz, "Live Episode! Starbucks: Howard Schultz," interview by Guy Raz, *How I Built This*, September 27, 2017, audio, http://one.npr.org/?sharedMediaId=551874532:554086519.

14. Nicolas Kachaner, Kermit King, Sam Stewart, "Four Best Practices for Strategic Planning," *Boston Consulting Group*, April 14, 2016, https://www.bcgperspectives.com/content/articles/strategic-planning-business-unit-strategy-four-best-practices-strategic-planning/#chapter1.

Chapter 10: INTERACTIVITY

1. Definition of interactive from Dictionary.com found at http://www.dictionary.com/browse/interact. Accessed on December 12, 2017.

Chapter 11: Relationships: Develop the Currency of the Future Organization

1. Liz Mineo, "Good Genes are Nice, but Joy is Better," *The Harvard Gazette*, April 11, 2017, https://news.harvard.edu/gazette/story/2017/04/over-nearly-80-years-harvard-study-has-been-showing-how-to-live-a-healthy-and-happy-life/.

2. Joshua Wolf Shenk, "What Makes Us Happy?" *The Atlantic*, June 2009, https://www.theatlantic.com/magazine/archive/2009/06/what-makes-us-happy/307439/.

3. Dan H. Fann, Jr., "Great Study Analyzes Normal Individuals," *The Harvard Crimson*, May 13, 1942, http://www.thecrimson.com/article/1942/5/13/grant-study-analyzes-normal-individuals-pin/.

4. Carolyn Gregoire, "The 75-Year Study that Found the Secrets to a Fulfilling Life," *Huffington Post*, August 11, 2013, http://www.huffingtonpost.com/2013/08/11/how-this-harvard-psycholo_n_3727229.html.

5. Carolyn Gregoire, "The 75-Year Study that Found the Secrets to a Fulfilling Life," *Huffington Post*, August 11, 2013, http://www.huffingtonpost.com/2013/08/11/how-this-harvard-psycholo_n_3727229.html.

6. JK Kiecolt-Glaser, TJ Loving, JR Stowell, WB Malarkey, S Lemeshow, SL Dickinson, R Glaser, "Hostile Marital Interactions, Proinflammatory Cytokine Production, and Wound Healing," *Archives of General Psychiatry* 62(12) (December 2005): 1377-1384. Found online at: https://jamanetwork.com/journals/jamapsychiatry/fullarticle/209153.
7. Armen Hareyan, "Isolated Heart Patients Have Twice the Risk of Dying, Present Challenges to Health Care Workers," *EmaxHealth*, April 13, 2004, http://www.emaxhealth.com/39/176.html.
8. Tom Rath and Jim Harter, "Your Friends and Your Social Well Being," *Gallup*, August 19, 2010, http://news.gallup.com/businessjournal/127043/friends-social-wellbeing.aspx.
9. Tom Rath and Jim Harter, "Your Friends and Your Social Well Being," *Gallup*, August 19, 2010, http://news.gallup.com/businessjournal/127043/friends-social-wellbeing.aspx.
10. No Author Found, "Every Move You Make," *The Economist*, August 20, 2008, http://www.economist.com/node/11957553.
11. No Author Found, "Every Move You Make," *The Economist*, August 20, 2008, http://www.economist.com/node/11957553.
12. No Author Found, "Every Move You Make," *The Economist*, August 20, 2008, http://www.economist.com/node/11957553.
13. Information about employee tenure was found in the Employee Tenure News Release from the Bureau of Labor Statistics, September 22, 2016, https://www.bls.gov/news.release/tenure.htm.

Chapter 12: Empathy: Use Emotional Intelligence to Move Others

1. Shazia Vegar Siddiqui, Ushri Chatterjee, Devvarta Kumar, Aleem Siddiqui, Nishant Goyal, "Neuropsychology of The Prefrontal Cortex," *Indian Journal of Psychiatry* 50(3), (July-September 2008): 202-208.
2. Mo Costandi, "Phineas Gage and the Effect of an Iron Bar Through the Head on Personality," *The Guardian*, November 8, 2010, https://www.theguardian.com/science/blog/2010/nov/05/phineas-gage-head-personality.

3. Mo Costandi, "Phineas Gage and the Effect of an Iron Bar Through the Head on Personality," *The Guardian*, November 8, 2010, https://www.theguardian.com/science/blog/2010/nov/05/phineas-gage-head-personality.
4. The definition of emotion found at Merriam-Webster at https://www.merriam-webster.com/dictionary/emotion, accessed on May 29, 2018.
5. "The Business Case For Emotional Intelligence," TalentSmart, updated 2009, https://www.talentsmart.com/media/uploads/pdfs/The_Business_Case_For_EQ.pdf.
6. Kalpana Srivastava, "Emotional Intelligence and Organizational Effectiveness," *Indian Journal of Psychiatry* 22(2): 97-99. Found online at https://www.ncbi.nlm.nih.gov/pmc/articles/PMC4085815/.
7. Daniel Goleman, Richard Boyatzis, Annie McKee, *Primal Leadership: Learning to Lead With Emotional Intelligence* (Boston: Harvard Business School Press, 2002), 250.

Chapter 13: Trust: Be Radically Transparent

1. Kevin Smith, "Here's the Confidential Memo Yahoo Sent Employees about Working from Home," *Business Insider*, February 23, 2017, http://www.businessinsider.com/yahoo-working-from-home-memo-2013-2.
2. Marissa Mayer, "Nostalgia, Gratitude, and Optimism," *Tumblr*, June 13, 2017, https://marissamayr.tumblr.com/post/161775943139/nostalgia-gratitude-optimism.
3. Richard Branson, "Give People the Freedom of Where to Work," *Virgin*, February 25, 2013, https://www.virgin.com/richard-branson/give-people-the-freedom-of-where-to-work#!.
4. Brené Brown, *Braving the Wilderness* (New York: Random House, 2017) 38.
5. Antoine Harary, David M Bersoff, Sarah Adkins, Steve Schmidt, Stephanie Lvovich, Gustavo Bonifaz, Kristin Heume, "2017 Edelman Trust Barometer - Global Report," *Edelman*, January 15, 2017, https://www.edelman.com/trust2017/.
6. "Confidence in Institutions," Gallup, accessed on November 10, 2017, http://news.gallup.com/poll/1597/confidence-institutions.aspx.

7. Chris Cillizza, "Americans Don't Trust Donald Trump. They Never Really Have," *CNN*, August 8, 2017, http://www.cnn.com/2017/08/08/politics/donald-trump-trust/index.html.

8. "2017 Work and Well Being Survey," American Psychological Association, May 24, 2017, http://www.apaexcellence.org/assets/general/2017-work-and-wellbeing-survey-results.pdf.

9. "Employee Distrust Is Pervasive in U.S. Workforce," American Psychological Association, April 23, 2014, http://www.apa.org/news/press/releases/2014/04/employee-distrust.aspx.

10. Susan Sorenson, "How Employee Engagement Drives Growth," *Gallup*, June 20, 2013, http://news.gallup.com/businessjournal/163130/employee-engagement-drives-growth.aspx.

11. Richard S. Wellins, Paul Bernthal, Mark Phelps, "Employee Engagement: The Key to Realizing Competitive Advantage," *DDI*, accessed on November 10, 2017, https://www.ddiworld.com/ddi/media/monographs/employeeengagement_mg_ddi.pdf?ext=.pdf.

12. Lesley Brown, "Keeping Employees Engaged," *Willis Towers Watson*, May 16, 2013, https://www.towerswatson.com/en/Insights/IC-Types/Ad-hoc-Point-of-View/2013/05/Keeping-Employees-Engaged?webSyncID=b28be412-e8a8-8ee7-7b2c-de5260185e9d&sessionGUID=02a82dbe-b623-5903-06a8-8c6a9e396048.

13. Lesley Brown, "Keeping Employees Engaged," *Willis Towers Watson*, May 16, 2013, https://www.towerswatson.com/en/Insights/IC-Types/Ad-hoc-Point-of-View/2013/05/Keeping-Employees-Engaged?webSyncID=b28be412-e8a8-8ee7-7b2c-de5260185e9d&sessionGUID=02a82dbe-b623-5903-06a8-8c6a9e396048.

14. Heather Boushey and Sarah Jane Glynn, "There are Significant Business Costs to Replacing Employees," *Center for American Progress*, November 16, 2012, https://www.americanprogress.org/wp-content/uploads/2012/11/CostofTurnover.pdf.

15. "Average Cost-Per-Hire for Companies Is $4,129, SHRM Survey Finds," Society for Human Resource Management, August 3, 2016, https://www.shrm.org/about-shrm/press-room/press-releases/pages/human-capital-benchmarking-report.aspx.

16. "Job Openings and Labor Turnover - September 2017," Bureau of Labor Statistics News Release, November 7, 2017, https://www.bls.gov/news.release/pdf/jolts.pdf.

17. Susan Sorenson, "How Employee Engagement Drives Growth," *Gallup*, June 20, 2013, http://news.gallup.com/businessjournal/163130/employee-engagement-drives-growth.aspx.

18. Paul J. Zak, "The Neuroscience of Trust," *Harvard Business Review*, January/February 2017, https://hbr.org/2017/01/the-neuroscience-of-trust.

19. Petula Dvorak, "She Flipped Off President Trump - and Got Fired from Her Government Contracting Job," *The Washington Post*, November 6, 2017, https://www.washingtonpost.com/local/she-flipped-off-president-trump--and-got-fired-from-her-government-contracting-job/2017/11/06/4cf1af9a-c2da-11e7-84bc-5e285c7f4512_story.html?utm_term=.281f8f719997.

20. Dan-Shang Wang and Chia-Chun Hsieh, "The Effect of Authentic Leadership on Employee Trust And Employee Engagement," *Social Behavior and Personality: An International Journal* 41 (May 2013): 613-624.

21. Etelka Lehoczky, "What If You Knew All Your Co-Workers' Salaries?" *Inc.*, May 2016, https://www.inc.com/magazine/201605/etelka-lehoczky/salary-transparency-company-strategy.html.

Chapter 14: PRODUCTIVITY

1. No sources cited.

Chapter 15: Expectations: Provide Abundant Clarity

1. Chris Wesseling, "Ben Roethlisberger Has Surgery to Repair Meniscus," *NFL.com*, October 17, 2016, http://www.nfl.com/news/story/0ap3000000722625/article/ben-roethlisberger-has-surgery-to-repair-meniscus.

2. Raine Sihvonen, M.D., Mika Paavola, M.D., Ph.D., Antti Malmivaara, M.D., Ph.D., Ari Itälä, M.D., Ph.D., Antti Joukainen, M.D., Ph.D., Heikki Nurmi, M.D., Juha Kalske, M.D., and Teppo L.N. Järvinen, M.D., Ph.D., for the Finnish Degenerative Meniscal Lesion Study (FIDELITY) Group, "Arthroscopic Partial Meniscectomy Versus Sham Surgery for a Degenerative Meniscal Tear," *New England Journal of Medicine*, 369 (December 2013): 2515-2524.

3. Raine Sihvonen, M.D., Mika Paavola, M.D., Ph.D., Antti Malmivaara, M.D., Ph.D., Ari Itälä, M.D., Ph.D., Antti Joukainen, M.D., Ph.D., Heikki Nurmi, M.D., Juha Kalske, M.D., and Teppo L.N. Järvinen, M.D., Ph.D., for the Finnish Degenerative Meniscal Lesion Study (FIDELITY) Group, "Arthroscopic Partial Meniscectomy Versus Sham Surgery for a Degenerative Meniscal Tear," *New England Journal of Medicine*, 369 (December 2013): 2515-2524.
4. Gareth Cook, "How the Power of Expectations Can Allow You to Bend Reality," *Scientific American*, October 16, 2012, https://www.scientificamerican.com/article/how-the-power-of-expectations-can-allow-you-to-bend-reality/.
5. Cara Feinberg, "The Placebo Phenomenon," *Harvard Magazine*, January/February 2013, https://harvardmagazine.com/2013/01/the-placebo-phenomenon.
6. Marco Nine, "Many Employees Don't Know What's Expected of Them at Work," *Gallup*, October 13, 2016, http://news.gallup.com/businessjournal/186164/employees-don-know-expected-work.aspx.
7. Maggie Overfelt, "What Millennials Want Most of All When Starting a New Job," *CNBC*, April 21, 2017, https://www.cnbc.com/2017/04/21/the-no-1-millennial-need-from-a-new-job-and-new-boss.html.
8. Karie Willard, "Millennials Want to Be Coached at Work," *Harvard Business Review*, February 27, 2015, https://hbr.org/2015/02/millennials-want-to-be-coached-at-work.

Chapter 16: Teams: Harness the Power of Future Teams

1. Adam Smith, *Wealth of Nations,* published in 1776. The first chapter talked about the Division of Labor.
2. Tiffany McDowell, Dimple Agarwal, Don Miller, Tsutomu Okamoto, Trevor Page, "Organizational Design: The Rise of Teams," *Deloitte*, February 29, 2016, https://dupress.deloitte.com/dup-us-en/focus/human-capital-trends/2016/organizational-models-network-of-teams.html#endnote-13.

3. Jeff Schwartz, Udo Bohdal-Spiegelhoff, Michael Gretczko, Nathan Sloan, "Global Human Capital Trends 2016," *Deloitte*, 2016, https://www2.deloitte.com/content/dam/Deloitte/global/Documents/HumanCapital/gx-dup-global-human-capital-trends-2016.pdf.

4. Tiffany McDowell, Dimple Agarwal, Don Miller, Tsutomu Okamoto, Trevor Page, "Organizational Design: The Rise of Teams," *Deloitte*, February 29, 2016, https://dupress.deloitte.com/dup-us-en/focus/human-capital-trends/2016/organizational-models-network-of-teams.html#endnote-13.

5. Tiffany McDowell, Dimple Agarwal, Don Miller, Tsutomu Okamoto, Trevor Page, "Organizational Design: The Rise of Teams," *Deloitte*, February 29, 2016, https://dupress.deloitte.com/dup-us-en/focus/human-capital-trends/2016/organizational-models-network-of-teams.html#endnote-13.

6. Wouter Aghina, Aaron De Smet, Kirsten Weerda, "Agility: It Rhymes with Stability," *McKinsey Quarterly*, December 2015, http://www.mckinsey.com/business-functions/organization/our-insights/agility-it-rhymes-with-stability.

7. Trevor Page, Amir Rahnema, Tara Murphy, Tiffany McDowell, "Unlocking the Flexible Organization," *Deloitte*, accessed on March 2, 2018, https://www2.deloitte.com/content/dam/Deloitte/global/Documents/HumanCapital/gx-hc-unlocking-flexible-%20organization.pdf.

8. Vikram Bhalla, Jean-Michel Caye, Andrew Dyer, Lisa Dymond, Yves Morieux, Paul Orlander, "High-Performance Organizations: The Secrets of Their Success," *Boston Consulting Group*, September 1, 2011, https://www.bcg.com/documents/file84953.pdf.

9. Aine Cain, "Jeff Bezos's Productivity Tip? The '2 Pizza Rule,'" *Inc.*, June 7, 2012, https://www.inc.com/business-insider/jeff-bezos-productivity-tip-two-pizza-rule.html.

Chapter 17: Training: Grow Your Greatest Asset

1. "2015 Industry Training Report," Training Magazine, November/December 2015, https://trainingmag.com/trgmag-article/2o15-training-industry-report.

2. "2015 Industry Training Report," Training Magazine, November/December 2015, https://trainingmag.com/trgmag-article/2o15-training-industry-report.
3. "ATD Releases 2016 State of the Industry Report," Association for Talent Development, News Release, December 8, 2016, https://www.td.org/insights/atd-releases-2016-state-of-the-industry-report.
4. Amy Adkins, "What Millennials Want from Work and Life," *Gallup*, May 11, 2016, http://news.gallup.com/businessjournal/191435/millennials-work-life.aspx.
5. Amy Adkins and Brandon Rigoni, "Millennials Want Jobs to Be Development Opportunities," *Gallup*, June 30, 2016, http://news.gallup.com/businessjournal/193274/millennials-jobs-development-opportunities.aspx.
6. Amy Adkins and Brandon Rigoni, "Millennials Want Jobs to Be Development Opportunities," *Gallup*, June 30, 2016, http://news.gallup.com/businessjournal/193274/millennials-jobs-development-opportunities.aspx.
7. "Two in Three Workers Quit Due to A Lack of Learning and Development Opportunities," total jobs.com press release, February 21, 2018, http://press.totaljobs.com/release/two-in-three-workers-quit-due-to-a-lack-of-learning-and-development-opportunities/.
8. Dan Schawbel, "Millennials Vs. Baby Boomers: Who Would You Rather Hire?" *Time*, March 29, 2012, http://business.time.com/2012/03/29/millennials-vs-baby-boomers-who-would-you-rather-hire/.
9. Dan Schawbel, "Millennials Vs. Baby Boomers: Who Would You Rather Hire?" *Time*, March 29, 2012, http://business.time.com/2012/03/29/millennials-vs-baby-boomers-who-would-you-rather-hire/.
10. Patrick Gillespie, "US has Record 6 Million Job Openings, Even as 6.8 Million Americans are Looking for Work," *CNN*, June 6, 2017, http://money.cnn.com/2017/06/06/news/economy/us-job-openings-6-million/index.html.
11. Laurence Bradford, "13 Tech Companies that Offer Cool Perks," *Fortune*, July 27, 2016, https://www.forbes.com/sites/laurencebradford/2016/07/27/13-tech-companies-that-offer-insanely-cool-perks/#1aec0a9679d1.

12. Lydia Dishman, "How the Gates Foundation Makes 52-Week Paid Parental Leave Work," *Fast Company*, April 26, 2018, https://www.fastcompany.com/40563031/how-the-gates-foundation-makes-52-week-paid-parental-leave-work.

13. "Embracing a Broader Definition of Well-Being," National Business Group on Health, March 2017, https://www.businessgrouphealth.org/pub/?id=ABA1E86C-782B-CB6E-2763-5DE483D2C2EF.

14. Natalie Hackbarth, Aaron Brown, Henry Albrecht, "Workplace Well-Being," *Quantum Workplace*, accessed on November 24, 2017, https://www.quantumworkplace.com/hubfs/Website/Resources/PDFs/Workplace-Well-Being.pdf.

15. Natalie Hackbarth, Aaron Brown, Henry Albrecht, "Workplace Well-Being," *Quantum Workplace*, accessed on November 24, 2017, https://www.quantumworkplace.com/hubfs/Website/Resources/PDFs/Workplace-Well-Being.pdf.

16. Information about Starbucks College Achievement Plan was found at https://www.starbucks.com/careers/college-plan, accessed on March 3, 2018.

Chapter 18: Organization: Establish a Robust System of Organization

1. George L. Kelling and James Q. Wilson, "Broken Windows," *The Atlantic*, March 1982, https://www.theatlantic.com/magazine/archive/1982/03/broken-windows/304465/.

2. George L. Kelling and James Q. Wilson, "Broken Windows," *The Atlantic*, March 1982, https://www.theatlantic.com/magazine/archive/1982/03/broken-windows/304465/.

3. George L. Kelling and James Q. Wilson, "Broken Windows," *The Atlantic*, March 1982, https://www.theatlantic.com/magazine/archive/1982/03/broken-windows/304465/.

4. George L. Kelling and James Q. Wilson, "Broken Windows," *The Atlantic*, March 1982, https://www.theatlantic.com/magazine/archive/1982/03/broken-windows/304465/.

5. Raghuram G. Rajan and Julie Wulf, "The Flattening Firm: Evidence from Panel Data on the Changing Nature of Corporate Hierarchies," *National Bureau of Economic Research,* Working Paper No. 9633, April 2003, http://www.nber.org/papers/w9633.pdf.
6. Raghuram G. Rajan and Julie Wulf, "The Flattening Firm: Evidence from Panel Data on the Changing Nature of Corporate Hierarchies," *National Bureau of Economic Research,* Working Paper No. 9633, April 2003, http://www.nber.org/papers/w9633.pdf.
7. Gary L. Neilsen and Julie Wulf, "How Many Direct Reports?" *Harvard Business Review*, April 2012, http://www.harvardbusiness.org/sites/default/files/How_Many_Direct_Reports.pdf.
8. Gary L. Neilsen and Julie Wulf, "How Many Direct Reports?" *Harvard Business Review*, April 2012, http://www.harvardbusiness.org/sites/default/files/How_Many_Direct_Reports.pdf.
9. "Work Management Survey 2015," Wrike, Inc., 2015, https://cdn.wrike.com/ebook/Wrike-Work-Management-Report-2015.pdf?utm_source=email&utm_medium=report&utm_campaign=2015&mkt_tok=eyJpIjoiWm1RNFl6Vm1Namc0WldWbSIsInQiOiJkelZPSFZtbXQzdEVWXC9yZVwvYVdINzlKMFZ6ckRqMTJETnl2RDRXWDAyU1JyMTVWanRUY1R1VW51bDBoM05ScFVx.
10. "Work Management Survey 2015," Wrike, Inc., 2015, https://cdn.wrike.com/ebook/Wrike-Work-Management-Report-2015.pdf?utm_source=email&utm_medium=report&utm_campaign=2015&mkt_tok=eyJpIjoiWm1RNFl6Vm1Namc0WldWbSIsInQiOiJkelZPSFZtbXQzdEVWXC9yZVwvYVdINzlKMFZ6ckRqMTJETnl2RDRXWDAyU1JyMTVWanRUY1R1VW51bDBoM05ScFVx.
11. "The Costs Associated with Disorganization," Brother International Corporation, 2010, http://www.brother-usa.com/Ptouch/MeansBusiness/whitepaper.pdf.
12. "The Costs Associated with Disorganization," Brother International Corporation, 2010, http://www.brother-usa.com/Ptouch/MeansBusiness/whitepaper.pdf.
13. David Allen dives deep on organization in his book, *Getting Things Done*. I strongly encourage you to purchase a copy.

14. Stephanie McMains and Sabine Kastner, "Interactions of Top-Down and Bottom-Up Mechanisms in Human Visual Cortex," *The Journal of Neuroscience* 31, No. 2 (January 2011): 587-597.

Chapter 19: Summary

1. No sources cited.

Chapter 20: Future Leader Quick Start Guide

1. No sources cited.

Chapter 21: Month 1: Take the Future Leader Assessment

1. No sources cited.

Chapter 22: Month 2: Get Insanely Organized

1. No sources cited.

Chapter 23: Month 3: Renew the Mission

1. No sources cited.

Chapter 24: Future Months: Create a Success Plan

1. No sources cited.

Index

absenteeism, 24
accessibility, 170
accountability, 142, 166, 168, 171, 180. See also transparency
Achievers, 18–19
adjacent possible, 47–49, 56
AI industry, 55, 99
Allen, David, 210
Amazon, 61, 92–93, 99
American Management Association, 94
American Psychological Association, 152
amplification, of ideas, 78–79
amplification, of transgressions, 155
analytical skills, 94–95
Archimedes, 65
Arthur Andersen, 13
Asana, 181, 193, 208–9
ASOS, 77, 80, 81–82
Association for Talent Development, 191
attire, attitudes toward, 42

attitudes, shaping of, 33–35

automation, xiv–xv, 53, 54–56, 108–9

aviation industry, simultaneous advancement and, 49–51, 55–56

Baby Boomers: boredom and, 15; communication preferences, 40–41; decline of, 4, 5–6, 8; defined, xiii–xiv, 4, 32–33; emotional intelligence and, 141–42; influence of, 4, 36–37, 216; institutional knowledge and, 38–39; Millennials vs., 5–6, 40–43; motivation and, 177; promotions and, 41; relationship building and, 128–29; retirement of, xiii, 38, 39, 108, 192, 216; statistics and surveys of, 15, 38, 39, 40–41, 128

Basecamp, 181, 208–9

Berdik, Chris, 165

big data, 92

Bill & Melinda Gates Foundation, The, 193

Bock, Arlie, 123–24

Boeing, 50

boredom, 14–16, 23, 54, 166, 192

Boston Consulting Group, 53

Bradberry, Travis, 138, 139–40, 143

Branson, Richard, 151

bravery, 84, 86, 159

Braving the Wilderness (Brown), 151

"Broken Windows" theory, 203–5

Brother International, 207–8

Brown, Brené, 151

burnout, 21, 22, 23, 216

calendars, as organizational tool, 211

Center for American Progress, 25, 154

change, embracing of, 43

Changi International Airport, 55–56

childhood experiences, 33–35

clothing, attitudes toward, 42

Clutch, 17–18

clutter, organization and, 212

CNN Money, 53

communication: directness, 159; face-to-face, 40–41, 129–31; interactivity and, 119–121; of mission, 83, 85, 166–69, 184–85; preferences for, 40–41, 129–31, 179; speeding up of, 179–80; statistics and surveys, 40–41; of strategy, 114; transparency and, 157–58, 169; trust and, 158. See also feedback; social media

compensation, unfair, 21

conferences, 106–7

confrontation, 127, 130–31

connection/disconnection, 155–56

Costco, 59–62

courage, leadership and, 82

creativity, 71–72, 161, 218. See also mission; strategy; synthesis

critical thinking skills, 95–98

cross-functional teams, 75, 180

culture, organizational, 21–23

data collection, 72, 85, 89–101

DDI, 153

decision-making framework, 80–83

dedication, vacation time and, 22–23

Deloitte, 178–79

disengagement. See engagement/disengagement

disorganization, 205–13, 239–45

distributed teams, 181–82

division of labor, 176

Donald, Jim, 103

"double-hatting," 207
Duke University, 125
dynamism, 109, 113, 115–16

Edelman Trust Barometer, 20, 152
EMC, 91
emotional intelligence (EI), 137–47, 158, 184
Emotional Intelligence 2.0 (Bradberry), 138, 143
empathy, 137–47, 158, 184
engagement/disengagement, 14–16, 23, 24–25, 153–54, 195
Enron, 13
ETS, 94
evaluation, 114–15
events, defining, 33–35
expectations, 16–17, 23, 163–73. See also feedback
EY, 20

face-to-face communication, 40–41, 129–31
feedback, 17–18, 23, 113–14, 130–31, 166, 170–72, 216
Feltman, Charles, 151
Ferris Bueller's Day Off (film), 31
Feuer, Michael, 11–12
flattening hierarchies, 180–81, 206–7, 208
flexibility, leadership and, 86, 109, 113, 115–16, 199
flexible hours, 41, 42
footprint, strategy and, 105
force, defined, xiii–xv, 38, 56
4 Disciplines of Execution, The (McChesney), 19
friction, relationship building and, 127, 130–31
functional teams, 75, 178–80

Future Leadership Framework: defined, xii, 9–10, 67, 218–19; quick start guide, 221–56. See also creativity; interactivity; leadership; productivity

Future Workplace, 21

Gage, Phineas, 137–39

Gallup poll, 15, 18, 125, 152

generational churn, 3–10, 29–43; defined, 4, 32–33, 38, 43; emotional intelligence and, 141–42; as external agent, xiii–xvi, 108; force of, 5–6, 10, 26–27, 38–43, 208–9, 216; generational influence, 36–37; generational preferences, 128–29; patterns/patternicity and, 29–32; relationship building and, 128–29; as roller coaster, 4; shaping of attitudes and values, 33–35. See also specific generation

Generation X: defined, 4, 32–33; influence of, 37; relationships and, 129

Generation Z: defined, 32–33; influence of, 37; motivation and, 177

geopolitical trends, 93

Getting Things Done (Allen), 210

Global Human Capital Trends (Deloitte), 178–79

globalization, 93

goals, importance of, 18–19, 23, 112, 166–67, 185

Goleman, Daniel, 140–41

Google, 181, 193

Grant Study, 123–24

Greaves, Jean, 143

Greenfield, Patricia, 95

Hammersley, Ben, 58

Harlow, John, 138–39

Harvard Business Review, 21, 143

healthcare costs, burnout and, 21

How Millennials Want to Work and Live (Gallup), 18

human inputs, technological vs., 59–62, 185–86

IBM Watson, 99

ideas, amplification of, 78–79

implementation, of mission, 82–83

"impressionable youth," 33–35

Industrial Psychiatry Journal, The, 140–41

institutional knowledge, 38–39

Intel, 45–46, 93

interactivity, 119–21, 161, 218–19. See also empathy; relationship building; trust

Internet, 37, 91–93, 179, 181, 185–86. See also social media

Jannus, Tony, 49

Johnson, Steven, 48

Kauffman, Stuart, 48

Kennedy, John F., 73–74

Kira Systems, 55

Kronos, 21

Kurzweil, Ray, 58

leadership: effects on productivity, 25; embracing change, 43; evolution of, 8–10; future leadership framework defined, xii, 9–10, 67, 218–19; leveraging the power of, 65–67, 217–20; measuring effectiveness of, 14–23, 27; playing the long game, 79–80, 113, 132–33, 186, 198, 219–20; quick start guide, 221–56; responsibilities of, 14; saying "I don't know," 158; skills focus, 65; underperforming, 24–26, 215–16; yesterday's vs. future, 87, 101, 117, 136, 147, 160, 173, 188, 201, 214

legal industry, 55

leverage, 65–67, 111, 180, 185–86, 217–18

life-span, company, 179

lists, as organizational tool, 209–11

Mannheim, Karl, 34, 37

manufacturing, technology and, 52–53

math skills, 94

matrix organizations, 180

Mayer, Marissa, 150

McDonnell Douglas, 50

McKinsey Quarterly, 93, 179

MetLife, 99

Millennials: analytical skills, 94; Baby Boomers vs., 5–6, 40–43; boredom and, 15, 166, 192; communication preferences, 40–41; connection of to mission, 84; defined, 4, 32–33; emotional intelligence and, 141–42; expectations and, 166; feedback and, 17–18, 170–71; influence of, 36–37; mission and, 84; motivation and, 177; as percentage of workforce, 39, 192; promotions and, 41; reading comprehension, 94; relationship building and, 128–29; rise of, xiii–xiv, 5–6, 38, 39, 129, 216; statistics and surveys of, 15, 17–18, 39, 40–41, 84, 94, 128, 166, 170–71, 191–92; tenure of, 128, 192; training of, 191–92

mission, 73–87; amplification of ideas and, 78–79; basic mistakes of, 80–83; cascade of, 111; clarity of, 74–80, 76, 81–82, 112, 166–67, 184–85; communication of, 83, 85, 166–69, 184–85; creation of, 84–86; creativity and, 72; as decision-making framework, 80–83; employee knowledge of, 18–19; examples of, 77–80; expectations and, 166–67; importance of, 18–19, 23, 80; Millennials and, 84; renewing of, 247–52; review of, 85–86; role of, 83; teams and, 111–12

MIT, 125–26

mobility, of work, 181–82

Moore, Gordon, 45–46, 47

Musk, Elon, 79–80

Namasté Solar, 157

NASA, 73–74

National Business Group on Health, 195

networks, size of, 125

New York Times (newspaper), 55
North American Leadership Conference, 106–7
Noyce, Bob, 45–46

Office 365, 181
OfficeVibe, 17
Ohio State University, 124
opportunity costs, 22
organization, improving, 203–14, 239–45
organizational culture, 21–23
organizational structure, 177–83, 206
outsourcing, 182, 198
overtime, 21, 23

patterns/patternicity, 29–32
"paying dues," 41
performance indicators, 110–11, 113, 114–15
perks, 193–95
personal competency, 139–40
personal connections, 155–56
Pheil, Abram, 49
Pittsburgh Steelers, 163–65, 172
praise, importance of, 171
"presentism," 58
Pressfield, Steven, 3
Primal Leadership (Goleman), 141
Princeton University, 212
"Problem of Generations" (Mannheim), 34
production mobility, 181–82

productivity: automation and, xiv–xv, 53, 54–56, 108–9; boredom and, 15; burnout and, 21; defined, 161–62, 219; disorganization and, 208; effects of relationship building on, 125–26; engagement and, 14–16, 20–21, 24, 153–54, 195; feedback and, 17; rapid technological development and, 51–56; statistics and surveys of, 24–25, 207–8; technology advancement and, 51–56; trust and, 20–21. See also expectations; organization; teams; training

profitability, 20–21, 24, 153–54, 194

Program for International Assessment of Adult Competencies, 94

project management, 207

promotions, 22, 41

pyramidical structure, 178–80

Qualtrics-Accel, 166

Quantum Workplace, 195

rapid technological advancement, 45–63; adjacent possible affects, 47–49, 56; as advantage, 98–100, 179; automation, xiv–xv, 53, 54–56, 108–9; as external agent, xiii, xiv–xvi; force of, 6–8, 10, 26–27, 56–62, 208–9, 217; human vs. technological inputs, 59–62, 185–86; nonlinear curve of advancement, 46–51, 47; productivity and, 51–56; relationships and, 129–31; simultaneous effort and, 49–51, 56

reading comprehension, 94

Real Time Statistics Project, 91

Reckard, Scott, 12

relationship building, 123–36; effective, 131–35; emotional intelligence (EI) and, 137–47; ending relationships, 134; facilitation of, 133; friction and, 127, 130–31; future of, 126–29; getting personal, 133; as long-term investment, 132–33; nurturing of, 132; people as people, 134; productivity and, 125–26; quality of, 124; size of networks, 125; technology and, 129–31; trust and, 131–32, 149–60. See also communication

relationship management, 140

resistance, defined, 3–4

resources, defining, 112
retirement, xiii, 38–39, 108, 128
retraining, strategy and, 105–6
robots, use of in manufacturing, 53
Roethlisberger, Ben, 163–65, 172

Sandberg, Sheryl, 4
scale, 178, 179, 180–83, 183–84
Schultz, Howard, 103–7
self-awareness, 140
self-management, 140
Silicon Valley, 149–50, 193–94
simultaneous effort, 49–51, 56
Skype, 181
Slack, 129–30
small businesses, 13, 182
Smith, Adam, 176
social competency, 139–40
social media, 120–21, 129–30, 157, 179, 181, 185–86
social networks, size of, 125
Society for Human Resource Management, 25, 154
SpaceX, 79–80
special projects, 207
speed, of growth, 179–80
Starbucks, 103–7, 198
statistics and surveys: analytical/reading skills, 94; automation, 55; communication preferences, 40–41; data generation/gathering, 91–93; decluttering, 212; employee boredom, 15, 166, 192; employee burnout, 21; employee engagement, 15, 24–25, 153–54; employee expectations, 16–17, 166; employee feedback, 17–18, 170–71; employee wellness programs,

195; Internet use, 37; job tenure, 40, 128, 192; job training, 191–92; job turnover, 21, 25–26, 153–54; juggling of long-term projects, 207; knowledge of employer's goals, 19; knowledge of employer's strategy, 19; knowledge of employer's vision or mission, 18–19; manufacturing sector, 52, 53; Millennials as percentage of workforce, 39, 192; mission connection, 84; network size, 125; number of open jobs, 192; organizational restructuring, 178–80, 206; productivity, 24–25, 207–8; relationship building, 123–24, 125–26; retirements, 38, 39; small businesses, 13; training expenditures, 191; trust, 20, 152–53, 156; use of vacation time, 22; workplace disorganization, 207–8

"stickiness," of teams, 184

stories, synthesis of data into, 72, 85, 89–101, 114

strategy, 103–17; communication of, 114; components of, 105–7; creativity and, 72; employee knowledge of, 19; evaluation of, 114–15; flexibility of, 109, 113, 115–16; footprint and, 105; importance of, 18–19, 23; improving skill of, 111–16; key performance indicators, 110–11, 113, 114–15; shifting winds and, 107–9; short and long term, 113; team-level, 111–16

structure, organizational, 177–83, 206

success: defining, xii, 75, 81; visualizing, 42, 112, 167, 185, 219–20

SWOT analysis, 112

synergy, 184

synthesis, 72, 85, 89–101, 114, 185

Taylor, Frederick Winslow, 207

teams, 175–88; building better, 183–87; cross-functional, 75, 180; functional, 75, 178–80; importance of, 176–77; mission and, 111–12; organizational progression and, 177–83; strategies for, 111–12, 113–14; technology and, 179, 181–82; trust and, 131–32; turnover and, 184, 186–87

technology: ability of to redefine, 6–8; advancement of, 46–51, 98–100, 179–82, 185–86, 208–9; effects on synthesis skills, 95; manufacturing and, 52–53. See also rapid technological advancement

TED, 77–79, 80

tenure, 40, 128, 192

time management, 65–67, 168, 217–18

Traditionalist, 32–33

training, 189–201

Training Magazine, 191

transgressions, amplification of, 155

transparency, 157–58, 169

travel industry, automation and, 55–56

Trello, 208–9

trust, 20–21, 131–32, 149–60

turnover: burnout and, 21; costs of, 25–26; interactivity and, 120; relationships and, 131, 135; speed of, xiv, 5–6; statistics and surveys, 21–22, 25–26, 153–54; structural, 5–6; teams and, 184, 186–87; training and, 195, 196; underperforming leadership and, 23–26, 216

Udemy, 15

uncertainty, embracing of, 98

underperformance, 24–26

U.S. Bureau of Labor Statistics (BLS), 38, 40, 52, 154

U.S. Small Business Association (SBA), 13

vacation time, 22–23

Vaillant, George, 124

vision, importance of, 18–19, 23, 111

VW, 13

wellness programs, 195

Wells Fargo, 11–13

Willis Towers Watson, 153

working hours, 41, 42

workload, 21, 23

Work Management Survey, 207
work spaces, 41, 181–82, 212
Wright brothers, 49–50

Yahoo!, 149–51

Zimbardo, Philip, 203–4
Zoom, 181

www.ingramcontent.com/pod-product-compliance
Lightning Source LLC
Chambersburg PA
CBHW060332220326
41598CB00023B/2689

* 9 7 8 0 9 9 9 8 1 3 6 0 7 *